I0554818

GOD ORDAINS MARRIAGES

Dr. Brenda Harper

COPYRIGHT

God Ordains Marriages
Dr. Brenda Harper
ISBN: 978-1-958356-28-9

Copyright © 1989
Current Edition Copyright © 2023

Printed in the United States

FOREWARD

I have been married to the love of my life for over forty-seven years! She has impacted my life in so many wonderful ways. During the early part of our marriage, the wonderful role she played in helping build a fulfilling life for our family was truly a blessing. My wife is my best friend and soulmate. The strong bond and relationship we share is a blessing from heaven!

'God Ordains Marriages' is a wonderful manuscript that will be very beneficial for anyone that applies these principles. I can attest that these principles, from our own experiences, work. I support the authenticity of this book. From the longevity of our labor, there have been many couples, singles, and divorcees that have benefited from the experiences of our marriage! If any readers follow these suggested principles in their own lives, there should be nothing they cannot conquer.

My wife is qualified to author this book because she has lived and experienced every word. She has counseled countless individuals. Testimony after testimony has proven that these biblical principles work! 'God Ordains Marriages' was generated through our testimony and experiences. One of our first action plans was asking God to be at the forefront of our marriage. Every situation in our marriage was an opportunity to conquer our mistakes and remain together in the fight for our union.

For any relationship to be successful, it will take both parties to work together on all issues within the marriage. Not all issues or problems will be resolved immediately. My wife and I work together constantly to keep harmony in our relationship and home, which was what inspired this book, 'God Ordains Marriages'!

I believe this book will continuously motivate readers to work on their marriage!

Bishop Andrew Harper

DEDICATION

Dear Bishop Andrew Harper,

I wanted to take a moment to express my deep gratitude and love for you. Our marriage has truly been a joyous occasion, filled with happiness and a sense of home. In my mind, marriage is intertwined with the magic charm of creating a loving and nurturing environment, and it encompasses all the beautiful and sacred aspects of our lives together.

To my dearest friend, my husband, the man I fell in love with long before time began, I want you to know that I believe our union was truly ordained by God. I feel blessed that heaven sent you to me as my friend and partner in life. The love and care you have shown me, in such an all-encompassing and forgiving manner, surpasses anything I have ever dreamed of. I am forever grateful to have you by my side.

I also want to express my gratitude to God for blessing us with our wonderful children: Eric, Marvin, Philip, Andrea,

Chariss, Alexis, and Christina. Our family has been a tremendous source of support throughout the journey of writing this book, "God Ordains Marriages." Their encouragement has been invaluable, and I feel incredibly blessed to have such a loving and caring family.

As I reflect on our family, and the completion of this project, I am reminded of the words from Acts 10:2: "He and all his family were devout and God-fearing; he gave generously to those in need and prayed to God regularly." I am forever indebted to God for His guidance and inspiration throughout this process.

Once again, to my dearest love Andrew, I want to thank you for being the pillar of love, friendship, and support in my life. Our journey together has been nothing short of extraordinary, and I am excited for the future that awaits us.

With all my love,

Dr. Brenda Harper

TABLE OF CONTENTS

GOD ORDAINS MARRIAGES...

COPYRIGHT..

FOREWARD.. I

DEDICATION III

INTRODUCTION 1

CHAPTER ONE 4

"LAYING THE FOUNDATION" 4

CHAPTER TWO 12

"THE UNION"..12

CHAPTER THREE...24

REDEMPTION RELATIONSHIP 24

CHAPTER FOUR...31

"VOWS" 31

CHAPTER FIVE...38

"FINANCES" 38

CHAPTER SIX 48

GEOGRAPHICAL LOCATION 48

CHAPTER SEVEN...57

"COMMUNICATION" 57

CHAPTER EIGHT 74

"SACRIFICES" 74

CHAPTER NINE 90

"FAITH, MARRIAGE, AND FAMILY" 90
PRIORITIZING SELF BEFORE PARENTHOOD: A PATH TO
PERSONAL FULFILLMENT 90

CHAPTER TEN 106

UNTIL DEATH, DO WE PART 106

"TESTIMONIES" 116

INDEX FOR FOUNDATIONS.............................119

ABOUT THE AUTHOR.....................................124

INTRODUCTION

The question of whether mankind truly comprehends, accepts, and embraces the knowledge that marriage is ordained by God is a profound one. In simple terms, the word 'ordained' means chosen or established by God.

However, the commercialization of traditional marriage ceremonies has often overshadowed the essence of the divine union that God intended. It is crucial for couples to ask themselves these important questions and examine their perceptions of the husband-wife relationship.

Does the husband perceive himself as a protector, provider, and caretaker, whose duties are instructed by God?

Does he understand the importance of following God's guidance in protecting and providing for his family?

Does he see himself loving his wife as Christ loves the church, leading his household while surrendering to divine leadership in both the spiritual and natural realms?

Likewise, as a wife, does her perception of marriage align with her husband's?

Is she prepared to reverence and obey her husband as the head of the family, subjecting and submitting herself to him?

Can she grasp the concept that God views her submission as a precious ornament and a great prize in His eyes?

Regrettably, there exist numerous perceptions of marriage that do not align with God as the ultimate authority who unites and ordains marriages. Many individuals may be unaware of the incredible blessings that God has in store for those marriages ordained by Him.

The purpose of this book is to assist those who are planning to get married, those who desire to be married, and those who are already married in understanding the divine nature of marriage as ordained by God.

Throughout my writing process, several questions arose, such as:

How many people truly recognize that marriage is ordained by God?

How many people comprehend the profound meaning behind the word 'ordained'?

When the marriage ceremony concludes and the vows, once stored in the hearts of a man and woman, are exchanged in the presence of clergy, friends, and family, does the couple possess the necessary tools *and* training to sustain the marriage they have entered?

In the following chapters, we will explore the profound concept of marriage as an ordained institution by God. We will delve into its spiritual significance, the roles of husband and wife as prescribed by God, and the blessings that flow from a union rooted in His divine plan.

It is our hope that everyone will gain a deeper understanding and appreciation for the sacredness of marriage as established and blessed by God Himself.

CHAPTER ONE

"Laying the foundation"

*L*ord, teach us to pray.

"And it came to pass, that as he was praying in a certain place, when he ceased, one of his disciples said unto him, Lord, teach us to pray, as John also taught his disciples. And he said unto them, when ye pray, say, Our Father which art in heaven, Hallowed be thy name. Thy kingdom comes. Thy will be done, as in heaven, so in earth. Give us day by day our daily bread. And forgive us our sins; for we also forgive everyone that is indebted to us. And lead us not into temptation; but deliver us from evil." (Luke 11:2-4, KJV).

This passage from the Bible describes a moment when Jesus was praying and one of His disciples asked him to teach them how to pray. Jesus then gives them the example of the 'Lord's Prayer' which is a request for divine guidance and instruction on how to pray. Prayer is very important in marriage. And prayer and forgiveness are essential to the endurance of a marital relationship.

What are some sins that come into a new marriage? Are we, as a couple, supposed to forgive all sins? If so, how do we forgive each other? Remember the word of God... *"For you should forgive each other 'seventy times seven times."* (Matthew 18:22, KJV), a number that symbolizes boundlessness.

> *"Forgiveness and love cover a multitude of faults, in a relationship" (Proverbs 10:12, AMP).*

While building your relationship with your spouse on the sure foundation of Jesus Christ (which is always the foundational prayer for our family), as one would with a personal relationship with Jesus Christ, please refer to this passage, *"upon this rock I will build my church"* (Matthew 16:13-18, KJV). Our perspective and interpretation of this passage is not only how it applies to our relationship with Christ, but also our relationships with family. It is also important to have a strong understanding of shared values and beliefs in one's relationship. As a couple, that foundation must be rooted in faith in Jesus Christ. (Matthew 16:13-18) The best time to build this foundation is either before marriage or in the early stages of marriage.

The early stage of marriage is the period immediately following the wedding. "Leave and cleave", is a biblical concept from Genesis 2:18-24 that refers to a new couple leaving behind their families and cleaving to one another. These two areas will be referred to throughout this book, as they signify the importance of solidifying these foundational truths as an individual and as a couple.

Here are some questions that came to mind while writing this section that I thought would be helpful to consider.

As a couple, how can we pray and surrender to God's role as our father and head of the marriage?

As the man, newly married and the head of the household, how do I individually, pray to God, regarding my roles; a man led by God, head of household, father, and protector of my family?

As the wife, how do I individually pray to God regarding my roles as a Godly woman, wife, submissive woman, and mother? How can my husband and I pray as a unit?

In the New Testament, God proclaims that whatever is bound on earth shall have been bound in heaven. Regarding God's view on the sanctity of marriage on earth, how will God's Will be done? How do we, as a couple, leave our families and cleave to each other when we are in need?

By building our relationship on a foundation of shared values, trust, and spiritual connection, we hope to find strength, support, and a deeper sense of purpose as we navigate through life's challenges. Matthew 16:19 adds a spiritual dimension to this analogy. By connecting this passage to building a relationship on a solid foundation, you will enhance your relationship through the divine principles that have the potential to unlock a deeper spiritual insight and provide blessings. This greater understanding of God's intentions for our lives, not only brings us closer to each other but also closer to our faith and our purpose. Here are a few key points to consider:

1. Clarity of Values: Faith provides a set of values and principles that can guide your actions and decisions. That gives you a sense of direction and helps you make choices that align with your beliefs.

2. Meaning and Purpose: Faith can offer a broader perspective on life's purpose. Believing in a higher power can lend to both joyful and challenging experiences, helping you see beyond the immediate circumstances.

3. Community and Belonging: Faith traditions come with a built-in community of like-minded individuals who share similar beliefs and values.

4. Hope and Resilience: Faith often instills a sense of hope and optimism, even in tough times. Believing in a divine purpose can provide comfort and resilience when facing adversity.

5. Guidance in Morality: Faith-based teachings often provide ethical guidelines and moral frameworks that help individuals navigate complex ethical dilemmas. This can lead to a stronger sense of personal integrity and ethical responsibility.

By building our relationship on this foundation, we believe that we can find strength and support during difficult times and deepen our understanding of God's plan for our lives. In addition, the idea of building our house on a solid foundation and joining *that* with being given the key to the kingdom (referencing Matthew 16:19), can be interpreted as finding a sense of purpose and fulfillment in life when you build your faith on a strong foundation.

Ultimately, the way everyone interprets and applies *these* teachings to their own lives is a personal matter, shaped by their own experiences and beliefs. Building a solid foundation in faith can bring a deeper sense of meaning and purpose to relationships and families. It can also help individuals navigate life's challenges with greater resilience and strength.

"I understand as a wife, that Ephesians 5:23 is an important scripture when keeping my husband in prayer. My duty as a wife, in submission to my husband as the head of our family, is to take care of him in every area of our union."

It is important to note that the concept of submission can be interpreted and applied in different ways, and it is up to each person to discern how it aligns with their own values and beliefs. Some may interpret it as a call to be obedient to their husband's authority, while others may see it as an invitation to serve and support their spouse in a partnership of mutual respect and love.

Whatever one's interpretation may be, seeking God's direction and aligning one's prayers with His principles is always a valuable practice in any aspect of life, including marriage. It is important for couples to communicate openly and work together to build a strong foundation; one of trust, respect, and love in their relationship, can help them grow together in life with grace and wisdom.

Nevertheless, healthy relationships involve mutual support and respect for each other's autonomy and freedom. It is essential to understand that supporting someone does not mean trying to control their actions or decisions. Encouraging your spouse to grow and pursue their goals while also respecting their choices is crucial for a healthy and fulfilling relationship. Ultimately, trust, communication, and mutual respect are the fundamentals of a strong and supportive relationship.

This covers all aspects, including sharing financial information; past and present. This poses the questions … What are some financial struggles in a new marriage? How do we pray and believe as one unit regarding God's provision concerning us? How do we realize, financially, that there is no more "me?"

You may consider this scripture, to begin with.

"And this is the confidence that we have toward him, that if we ask anything according to his will, he hears us."

(1 John 5:14, ESV)

Financial stress is often generated by individualism. As a result, some well-meaning individuals may end up living beyond their means. At times, we can find ourselves wanting what other people have, instead of seeing that we have all that we need. Financially, *the need* is taking care of one's living – *a desire* is taking care of their wants. For example, I want a Mercedes Benz because my neighbor has one.

Unfortunately, it causes people to compete with false hopes and desires, looking through the eyes of envy and strife. Regardless of the item(s), it is important to be patient, wait, and save. Do not put a financial stressor on the family. As a couple, it is important to save together and to create instant, long-term, and middle-term goals. Do not put unnecessary stress on your finances and marriage.

CHAPTER TWO

"The Union"

It is important to have a strong understanding of knowledge and understanding in a relationship. This includes knowing about the bond you will share with your spouse, as well as understanding the spiritual aspect of your union. God plays a significant role in bringing soulmates together.

The book of Proverbs refers to encouraging people to trust in God and seek His guidance in all aspects of their lives. Faith is an important aspect of decision-making and relationships.

The book of Job emphasizes the importance of trusting in God's wisdom and sovereignty, even in challenging times. This can apply to relationships as well.

These thoughts are centered around the importance of faith and trust within your relationships. By trusting in God and seeking His guidance, you can reinforce the foundation for your union and weather any storms that come your way.

God reminded Job, in the larger scheme of things, encouraged him to let go of his own sense of control and to submit to God's plan for his life.

Let me summarize and provide some insights on this matter:

Firstly, couples should ask themselves, "Are we truly in love and committed to each other? "And "Are we marrying the right person? These questions are important to ask before entering your marriage. It allows you to commit to one another with a sense of certainty and a deep understanding of your spouse.

Secondly, preparation for marriage should ideally begin with a focus on the developmental process. This includes developing skills such as communication, problem-solving, and emotional regulation which are crucial for a successful marriage.

Thirdly, the act of getting married is what makes a couple truly married, regardless of whether they have a formal wedding ceremony or not. The primary focus should be on the commitment to each other rather than the external trappings of the wedding.

In sharing the ancient belief of a Christian ceremony and how it is proper for believers who are getting married (which is based on the idea that marriage in Christ Jesus is more than just a contract, but rather a profound unity between two individuals that is ordained by God), early Christians understood that the significance of marriage and finding a spouse was considered a 'good thing' and favor from the Lord. Note that modern society may not view marriage in the same way, with many people accepting common-law marriages and not seeing the spiritual basis of marriage.

However, this foundational belief is centered around the idea that marriage is a spiritual union that should be ordained by God through a Christian ceremony. This reflects a strong commitment to one's faith and the belief that God should play the central role in one's marriage.

It is important to recognize that marriage is a significant and sacred union, regardless of one's religious beliefs. A strong and healthy marriage requires an emphasis based on mutual respect, trust, and commitment from both parties. Self-evaluation and personal growth are essential components for building a successful relationship. Each person must be willing to work on their own issues and be open to constructive criticism *and* feedback from their spouse.

While religious beliefs can provide a framework for understanding the spiritual significance of marriage, it is not the only path to a successful union. It is important to respect and acknowledge the diverse beliefs and values of individuals and couples.

A scripture in Corinthians speaks of the importance of shared faith and commitment to Christ in marriage. It is important to remember, however, that not all couples may share the same beliefs, and that does not necessarily mean their marriage is doomed to fail.

Ultimately, the success of a marriage depends on the dedication and effort of both parties. By prioritizing open communication, mutual respect, and a commitment to personal growth, couples can build a strong and enduring relationship, regardless of their religious beliefs.

"We have personal experiences with these beliefs of which I am speaking. The experiences with these beliefs put my husband and I in a unique position to provide some insights – based on historical and cultural contexts."

The institution of marriage is indeed traced back to the biblical creation story in <u>Genesis</u>. It is a sacred covenant between two individuals, and in Christian teachings, it is regarded as a reflection of the relationship between Christ and the church. Marriage requires commitment, sacrifice, and love from both individuals, and it is a process of growth and development.

This beautiful passage from the Book of Genesis, in the Bible, speaks of the belief that humans were created in the image of God and that both men and women were given a special blessing to be fruitful and multiply. It highlights the importance of valuing and respecting all human life. It speaks of the idea that we all have a special role to play as husband and wife. (Genesis, KJV)

While God instituted the institution of marriage, it is important to acknowledge that cultural and societal norms have also influenced the way marriage is perceived and practiced. Therefore, it is important to approach marriage with a sense of reverence and understanding of its sacredness, while also being mindful of the cultural and societal contexts in which it exists.

A healthy and successful marriage requires dedication, communication, and mutual respect from both parties. Whether rooted in religious beliefs or not, the institution of marriage serves as a foundation for building strong and enduring relationships.

The wedding in Cana of Galilee is indeed a significant event in Christian teachings, as it marks the first public miracle performed by Jesus. The miracle of turning water into wine was a symbol of Christ's power and presence in the marriage, and it is often interpreted as a sign of God's approval and blessing on the union.

Furthermore, while the presence of Jesus at a wedding may not be a physical reality for every couple, it is important to remember that His teachings and example can serve as a guiding force in the marriage. His message of love, forgiveness, and sacrifice can inspire couples to approach their union with humility, patience, and compassion, and to strive for a relationship that is rooted in faith and spiritual growth.

"It is wonderful to know after all these years that we have found a way to incorporate God's plan into our relationship and that it has brought a positive change to our lives."

Seeking guidance and direction from a higher power can bring a sense of peace and purpose to one's life and can also help individuals to gain a better understanding of themselves and their relationships.

It is also common for people to look back on their past and realize they were lacking certain knowledge or understanding that they have gained through their experiences and growth. It is a sign of personal development and growth to recognize areas where you once lacked knowledge and to strive to improve upon them.

It is also important to continue seeking wisdom and guidance from God and to remain open to learning and growing in all aspects of your life, especially your relationships. May God continue to bless and guide you on your journey.

While financial limitations can be a challenge for many couples today, it is important to remember that the true value of a wedding lies not in the extravagance of the celebration, but in the commitment and love between the couple. It is possible to have a beautiful and meaningful wedding without breaking the bank, and it is important for couples to prioritize what is truly important to them in the celebration.

While developing a relationship, it is vital to consider financial issues:

Yes, it is crucial to consider financial matters when developing a relationship, especially if you plan on making a long-term commitment to each other. As I mentioned earlier, financial problems can cause significant stress and strain on any relationship.

It is important to have open and honest communication about your financial situation, including debts, income, and expenses. Discussing financial goals and developing a plan to achieve them can help you both work together toward financial stability.

In addition, it is essential to have a similar approach to money management. Some couples choose to combine their finances, while others prefer to keep their finances separate.

Whatever approach you choose, make sure that you are both on the same page and understand each other's habits and attitudes toward money.

Remember that developing a strong financial foundation for your relationship takes time and effort, but it is worth it in the long run. With careful planning, communication, and a willingness to work together, you can overcome financial challenges and build a secure future together.

Again, financial issues can bring a significant source of stress in any relationship, and it is important to address them early on. As I mentioned, budgeting for the home is crucial, especially in the early stages of a marriage.

Creating a budget can help you keep track of your expenses and ensure that you are living within your means. It is also essential to communicate openly and honestly about your financial situation, including any debts you may have. This will help you both work together to develop a plan for paying off any outstanding debts and avoiding future financial problems.

In addition to budgeting and communication, it can also be helpful to seek guidance from financial advisors or counselors. They can provide you with the tools and resources you need to make informed decisions about your finances and develop a plan for long-term financial stability.

Remember that financial issues can be challenging, but with open communication, careful planning, and a willingness to work together, you can overcome them and build a strong and stable core for your future together.

Building a strong and stable foundation for your future is important in life, especially in relationships. A strong foundation can help to establish trust, communication, and a sense of shared values and goals. This foundation can also help to weather any challenges or conflicts.

Some examples of building a strong foundation include:

Establishing open and honest communication:
Communication is key to any healthy relationship. Being able to express your thoughts and feelings openly and honestly can help to build trust and understanding between individuals.

Setting shared goals and values: It is important to have a sense of shared values and goals with your spouse, as this can help to create a sense of unity and purpose.

Resolving conflicts in a healthy way: Conflict is a normal part of any relationship, but it is important to learn how to resolve conflicts in a healthy and respectful way. This can help to prevent resentment and build trust.

Spending quality time together: Spending time together doing things you both enjoy can help to create positive memories and build a sense of intimacy.

Supporting each other: Supporting each other through both the good times and the bad can help to build a sense of partnership and trust.

Building a strong and stable foundation in a relationship takes time, effort, and a commitment to open communication and shared values.

It is common for people to seek guidance and direction from their faith and religious beliefs, including in matters of relationships. Some couples seek God's guidance and wisdom, which can provide a sense of clarity and purpose in their relationships. However, it is important to note that not everyone shares the same beliefs, and there are many ways to approach relationships and seek guidance.

The principles and values that guide our lives and relationships are deeply personal and can come from a variety of sources, including religious teachings, personal experiences, and cultural traditions. It is up to everyone to determine what principles and values resonate with them and to seek guidance and support as they navigate through their own lives.

It is important to note that every marriage is unique and there are no one-size-fits-all solutions. But there are proven universal principles that help couples build strong and healthy relationships. These principles include effective communication, mutual respect, trust, honesty, empathy, and the ability to compromise.

Effective communication is key to a healthy marriage. Couples should take time to listen to each other and express their thoughts and feelings openly and honestly. You should also learn to communicate in a respectful and non-judgmental way, avoiding blame and criticism.

Mutual respect is also important in a marriage. Couples should value each other's opinions and feelings and treat each other with kindness and consideration while avoiding disrespecting each other or engaging in behaviors that undermine the relationship.

Trust is another crucial element of a healthy marriage. Be honest and transparent with each other and avoid keeping secrets or hiding information. You should also avoid behaviors that erode trust, such as lying or cheating.

Empathy is also important in a marriage. Couples should try to understand each other's perspectives and feelings and offer support and encouragement when needed. They should also be willing to put themselves in their mate's shoes and consider how their actions may impact one another.

Finally, the ability to <u>compromise</u> is essential in a marriage. All couples should be willing to find solutions that work for both and avoid getting stuck in a pattern of conflict or argument. And be willing to make sacrifices and put the needs of the relationship above your desires.

Overall, building a healthy and strong marriage requires effort, commitment, and a willingness to work through challenges and difficult times. With these principles in mind, couples can create a fulfilling and loving relationship that stands the test of time.

"Faith and spirituality can play a significant role in our marriage while providing us with comfort, guidance, and a sense of purpose. Whether we find solace in a higher power or in the relationships we have with loved ones, it is important to acknowledge and appreciate the blessings that come our way."

May your marriage be filled with love, joy, and blessings.

CHAPTER THREE

Redemption Relationship

I n Christian theology, redemption refers to the act of
God restoring humanity to a right relationship with
Him through the sacrifice of Jesus Christ on the cross.
This redemption is not limited to the individual's spiritual
life but extends to all areas of life, including marriage.

The idea of a redemptive relationship in marriage refers
to the restoration of the marriage relationship to its original
and intended state, which was damaged by sin. This
redemption involves forgiveness, healing, and restoration of
the relationship between husband and wife. In Ephesians,
the Apostle Paul emphasizes the importance of husbands
loving their wives in the same way that Christ loved the
Church and gave himself up for it.

*"Husbands, love your wives, even as Christ also loved
the church, and gave himself for it;" (Ephesians 5:25)*

The incarnation of Jesus Christ, which refers to God taking on human flesh, is a vital aspect of God's redemptive plan for humanity. By becoming fully human while remaining fully divine, Jesus was able to identify with humanity's struggles and temptations and offer himself as the perfect sacrifice for sin. Through His death and resurrection, Jesus made redemption and reconciliation possible for all who believe in him.

Therefore, Christians understand redemption as not only a spiritual reality but a practical reality that affects all areas of life, including marriage. The redemptive relationship and reconciliation in marriage reflect the grace and love that God has shown us through His redemption plan.

Let us reflect on the concept of a redemptive relationship in marriage, which typically refers to the idea that a couple can find healing, restoration, and renewal in their relationship through forgiveness, grace, and a commitment to growth and transformation.

In a redemptive relationship, couples will recognize that they are not perfect and that they will inevitably make mistakes or hurt each other. They also believe that there is hope for healing and restoration through a process of repentance, forgiveness, and reconciliation.

This can involve acknowledging and taking responsibility for one's actions, seeking forgiveness from one's spouse, and working together to rebuild trust and restore the relationship. It will involve seeking support from trusted individuals or professionals, such as pastors or counselors.

Redemptive relationships in marriage are grounded in a deep sense of love, compassion, and grace. Rather than focusing on blame, criticism, or punishment, couples in redemptive relationships seek to understand and empathize with one another's perspectives and work together towards a shared vision for their future. The goal of a redemptive relationship is to create a marriage that is not only strong and resilient, but also reflective of the transformative power of love, forgiveness, and grace.

It is common for couples to experience disagreements or conflicts in their relationship - even if they love each other deeply. It is important to acknowledge that differences in opinion are natural and healthy in any relationship, and that communication is key to resolving them. Effective communication involves active listening, empathy, and a willingness to compromise. It is important to approach conversations with an open mind and avoid becoming defensive or dismissive of your spouse's concerns. Working together to find common ground and solutions can strengthen the relationship and build trust.

Remember in any relationship, it is important to recognize that change is inevitable. Couples may experience challenges as they adapt to new circumstances, such as career changes, moving to a new location, or starting a family. Maintaining a strong foundation of communication and mutual respect can help couples navigate these transitions together.

A successful relationship depends on the commitment and effort of both mates. While it is important to prioritize the relationship and work towards harmony, it is also important to recognize that no relationship is perfect, and that forgiveness and grace are essential to moving forward.

In a redemptive relationship, love goes beyond just a feeling or emotion. It involves sacrificial actions, putting the needs of the other person before your own, and being willing to forgive and reconcile. This type of love is exemplified in the relationship between Jesus and His followers and can also be applied in a marital relationship.

Marriage provides a unique opportunity for spouses to practice redemptive love daily. This can involve sacrificing personal desires, forgiving past hurts, and working towards the betterment of the relationship. By doing so, couples can become more united and reflect the love of Christ in their relationship. It is important to note that redemptive love does not mean accepting or condoning harmful behavior. Rather, it involves working towards healing and reconciliation in a relationship. This may involve setting boundaries, seeking outside help, and addressing any underlying issues.

Redemptive relationships involve sacrificial love, forgiveness, and a willingness to put the needs of the other person before your own. By practicing these principles in a marriage, couples can become more united and reflect the love of Christ in their relationship.

Prayer is indeed an important aspect of a healthy relationship, as it allows couples to seek guidance and wisdom from God. Putting others before ourselves and being willing to compromise are also important principles to practice in a marriage.

God should be the mediator in any union, and we should depend on Him for all aspects of our lives, including marriage. It is important to invest time and effort into our relationships and to build a strong foundation that will keep our marriages secure.

Our analogy about building a house on a strong foundation serves as a reminder that investing in the unseen aspects of marriage (such as communication, trust, and commitment) can lead to a strong and lasting relationship.

Prayer is a powerful tool in any relationship, and it is especially important in a Christian marriage. The book of Thessalonians reminds us, we should pray without ceasing, and allow the Holy Spirit to guide our prayers according to God's Will.

Pray without ceasing. In everything give thanks: for this is the will of God in Christ Jesus concerning you.

(1 Thessalonians 5:17-19 KJV)

In a marriage, prayer can help couples to better understand each other's needs, desires, and struggles. It can also provide strength and comfort during difficult times to help foster a deeper sense of unity and intimacy within the relationship.

As we pray for our spouses and seek to understand their hearts, we can grow in empathy and compassion toward them. As we pray for God's guidance and wisdom in our marriage, we learn to trust in IIis plan and seek to follow IIis will.

Overall, prayer is an essential aspect of any Christian marriage and can help couples to grow in love, unity, and understanding.

"My husband says I am his Angel from heaven...

It is heartwarming to hear such loving words from my husband. We share a special bond and appreciation for one another. We are grateful for the people in our lives and recognize the blessings that come our way from heaven."

This can be a great source of comfort, and joy for all couples who recognize such blessings. It is wonderful to acknowledge the role that faith and spirituality can play in our lives and relationships.

CHAPTER FOUR

"Vows"

This chapter places a focus on making a vow and fulfilling your vow in a timely manner to God, your spouse, children, extended family and friends, and your ministry. When entering marriages that are ordained by God, there are specific details that require close attention, such as the vows that are being made. Marriage vows are sacred promises made between two individuals, in the presence of God, to love and honor each other, to remain faithful, and to support each other through all circumstances.

It is essential to pay close attention to the words that are being spoken during the marriage ceremony and to understand the commitment that is being made. The vows made during a marriage ceremony should be taken seriously and fulfilled with sincerity and devotion.

In addition, couples should seek God's guidance and wisdom in their marriage and strive to fulfill their vows with the help of His grace and strength, regardless of the size or significance of the job at hand: financial limitations, geographical location, educational background, ministry attendance, family responsibilities or plans. Seeking God's divine guidance and instruction is crucial.

I suggest that you should always rely on God's wisdom and guidance in making decisions, no matter what challenges or circumstances you may face. We cannot emphasize enough the importance of trusting in God's guidance and direction in every aspect of life, regardless of your limitations or circumstances. Ultimately, seeking divine instruction and guidance is essential for making sound decisions that align with God's Will and purpose for your life.

The book of Ecclesiastes advises us to be careful when making vows to God and to fulfill them promptly. It emphasizes the importance of keeping our promises to God and he warns us against making vows that we cannot keep.

Making empty promises to God is foolish and displeasing to Him. Instead, we should be careful and thoughtful when making vows to God and ensure that we fulfill them with sincerity and devotion. The passage reminds us that God takes our promises seriously, and we should always strive to keep our word to Him. (Ecclesiastes 5:4-5)

Many couples have heard the following statement "Dearly beloved, we are gathered here today, in the sight of God, and in the face of this company to join this man and woman in holy 'Matrimony'". Here, 'Matrimony' is referring to the Christian sacrament of marriage. The statement of making vows with sound wisdom and reverence comes from the Apostle Paul's letter to the Romans. In this passage, Paul is exhorting the Christian community to live in harmony with one another, to love one another, and to live peaceably with all men. He recommends that when making vows or promises, we should do so with sound wisdom, taking them seriously and with reverence for God. He advises that we should be discreet and sober-minded when making promises and should not take them lightly. This passage suggests that making vows is a serious matter and that we should approach it with caution, thoughtfulness, and a deep respect for God. By doing so, we demonstrate our commitment to honor God and to live in harmony with each other.

It is great to know that you have found guidance and direction in your relationship by following a plan based on your beliefs and values. Seeking wisdom and counsel from a source that aligns with your beliefs can be a helpful tool in navigating challenges and making decisions in your relationship. By taking responsibility for our own mistakes and seeking solutions through the principles of our faith, it helps us to build a stronger foundation for our relationship.

It is important to remember that relationships take work and effort. Seeking guidance from a higher power provides us with a sense of direction and purpose.

Romans 12:17-18 (KJV) Advises us to not seek revenge or retaliate when someone does us wrong. Instead, we should strive to do what is right and honorable in the eyes of everyone. Moreover, the passage urges us to live in peace with others as much as possible. It acknowledges that living in harmony with everyone may not always be achievable but encourages us to do our part in creating a peaceful and respectful environment.

"I am speaking from experience; my husband and I have tried it for ourselves regarding seeking God for guidance with every decision we had to make. As a couple, we rely on our abilities which are limited by God's abilities. As we abide in the flesh," we follow our own way of decision making. When we allow God to take over and direct us in every decision, God's divine Will becomes active, and we reap the benefits of His blessings."

Seeking God and allowing Him to guide every decision in a marriage is crucial for a successful and fulfilling relationship. When both partners prioritize their faith and allow the Holy Spirit to lead them, they will reap the benefits of a spiritual union. This requires a level of commitment and dedication, but it is worth it for the growth and maturity of the marriage. It is important to remember that marriage vows are not just made between two people, but also before God and the community of witnesses. Therefore, seeking God's guidance and abiding in the Spirit should be a central aspect of a Christian marriage.

In a marriage, it is often the small things that make a big difference. Simple gestures of kindness, such as taking the time to understand your spouse's thoughts and feelings before jumping to conclusions, or showing patience when working through problems, can go a long way in building a strong and healthy relationship. It is also important to remember that communication is key in any relationship, particularly in a marriage. Taking the time to talk to your spouse, actively listen to their perspective, and express your thoughts and feelings can help avoid misunderstandings and prevent conflicts from escalating. Overall, focusing on the little things and trying to be kind, patient, and understanding can help nurture a loving and fulfilling marriage.

An important thing to do in marriage is to communicate your appreciation, by letting your spouse know how much their love means to you!

"This has helped strengthen our bond and encourage more positive behavior."

It is great that you have learned about the importance of seeking God for guidance, fulfilling vows, and projecting a positive image as a saved couple. Indeed, these principles can be essential in maintaining a healthy and happy marriage. Remember that every marriage is unique, and what works for one couple may not necessarily work for another. It is crucial to communicate openly and honestly with your spouse, work together as a team, and continually strive to strengthen your relationship. As you continue your journey, may you find joy, love, and fulfillment in your marriage.

Remember, a healthy marriage is built upon mutual respect, love, and understanding, and it is the little things that we do for each other that can help sustain these qualities over time.

The book of 1 Corinthians is often referred to as the

"Love Chapter."

It describes the qualities of love, or "charity" as translated in the Bible. Love is patient and kind, not jealous or boastful. It is humble and considerate, putting the needs of others before its own. Love is slow to anger and does not hold grudges or think evil thoughts. It rejoices in truth and righteousness and can endure all things.

The highlights are important to the love in our lives and encourage us to strive for these qualities in our relationships with others. When we show love to others, we can create a more peaceful and harmonious world.

(1 Corinthians 13:4-7)

With this ring

CHAPTER FIVE

"Finances"

How we handle our money speaks volumes about what is really going on inside... The 'American way' today is buying things you do not need with money you do not have, to impress people you do not like." This quote by R. Kent Hughes suggests that our financial habits and decisions can reveal a lot about our values and priorities. The idea that people often spend money on unnecessary things to impress others is a commentary on the materialistic culture of modern society. Hughes implies that this tendency to prioritize social status and material possessions can distract us from more meaningful pursuits and relationships.

The phrase "The Gift of Giving" in the title of Hughes' book suggests that a more fulfilling way of using our resources might be to focus on helping others. Overall, this quote encourages reflection on our relationship with money and what it says about our inner values and motivations.

Financial planning and budgeting, whether single or married, are vital to a relationship. While it may be tempting to indulge in everything one desires, the reality is that budgeting is a necessary aspect of financial management. Any budgeting should be discussed and implemented prior to marriage to avoid financial strain and conflict. *There is more detailed information regarding discussing financial matters as a couple or potential couple in chapter seven.*

Living within one's means is an important key factor in successful budgeting. This means that expenses should not exceed income and that financial decisions should be made based on realistic financial resources.

I would like to emphasize the importance of responsible financial management and the need to prioritize budgeting in both single and or married life.

The word of God speaks of wise people who can accumulate wealth and valuable resources, such as oil, in their homes. It also speaks of how foolish individuals are likely to squander or waste these resources, without realizing their true value. (Proverbs 21:20, KJV)

This implies that being wise with one's resources is essential for financial success and stability. Accumulating wealth and resources is not enough - one must also be able to manage wealth effectively to reap the benefits.

In the context of personal finance, this word may be interpreted as a warning against overspending or living beyond one's means. If one has access to great riches and valuable resources, one must exercise wisdom and prudence in managing them to avoid losing them.

However, we encourage the cultivation of wisdom and fiscal responsibility to achieve long-term financial security and prosperity.

The highlights of the biblical concept of tithing involve giving a portion of one's income or resources to support religious organizations or causes. Tithing is a way of demonstrating faith and trust in God's provision and promises. Because God is our source.

The 'word' of God suggests that by bringing the whole tithe into the storehouse, one can experience blessings from God in the form of abundance and protection. It implies that tithing is not just a financial method but also a spiritual practice that can bring blessings and benefits beyond financial gain. (Malachi 3:10, KJV)

We can experience God's promises by faithfully tithing. As it is a form of worship and reinforcing our trust in Him, we will be able to see the results for ourselves. It has been said and proven many times, by moving in faith, you can't beat God in giving. By having faith in God's provision, tithing is a financial and spiritual practice that can bring blessings and benefits to individuals and their communities. This practice alone can encourage individuals to have faith in God's provision by faithfully giving and supporting any religious organizations or causes.

Several principles that contribute to financial stability in a marriage include tithing, trust, honesty, budgeting, agreement regarding spending, paying bills on time, and discipline. These principles are based on trust and belief that God is in control of one's personal and spiritual affairs, and that focusing on spiritual things is more important than material possessions.

As believers, one's financial decisions should be guided by faith and trust in God's provision and guidance. Christ can provide not just spiritual but also financial advice. By following His guidance, one can experience financial stability and blessings.

The emphasis is on the importance of spiritual values over material possessions, which suggests that the goal of financial stability is not just financial security, but also spiritual fulfillment and growth. So, aligning with the biblical teaching indicates that one cannot serve both God and money, and that one should seek first the kingdom of God and His righteousness. (Matthew 6:24,33, KJV)

We encourage believers and non-believers to trust in God's provision and to prioritize spiritual growth over material possessions.

The importance of setting one's heart and mind on spiritual things, rather than earthly things. It is suggested, that as believers, our goals should be to align one's thoughts and actions with God's Will and purpose. (Colossians 3:1-2, KJV)

By putting God first in all aspects of one's life, including finances, and giving God the first fruits of everything, we can demonstrate our faith and trust in God's provision and guidance.

While we are joined together as one, we are still individuals needing to have our own relationship with God. We also need to cultivate personal relationships with God *and* prioritize Him in our lives, while working together as a couple to honor God in our life.

An emphasis on prioritizing spiritual values and putting God first in all aspects of life, including finances. We encourage couples to work together on their relationship with God.

Material possessions are fleeting and can be lost or destroyed, but our relationship with God and others can provide lasting joy, fulfillment, and purpose. It is essential to prioritize our relationships with God and the people in our lives, as they are the ones that truly matter and can bring us a sense of contentment and peace.

Material possessions can also become a hindrance to our spiritual growth if we become too attached to them and prioritize them above our relationship with God. So, it is essential to keep a healthy perspective on material possessions and use them wisely to serve God and others.

We recognize the importance of communication when it comes to finances in a marriage. Money can indeed be a sensitive topic, and both individuals need to be transparent about their income and expenses.

As a couple, putting your income together can be a good way to ensure that you are both working towards and sharing your financial goals. This helps you better manage your expenses and avoid any potential conflicts that may arise from having separate finances.

It is important to note that there is no one-size-fits-all approach when it comes to managing finances in a marriage. Some couples may find that keeping separate accounts works best for them, while others may prefer having a joint account. It is up to each couple to determine what works best for their unique situation and level of comfort.

Regardless of how you choose to manage your finances, maintaining trust and open communication is crucial. Regularly checking in with each other about your financial situation and working together to create a budget and savings plan can help ensure that you are both on the same page and working towards a secure financial future.

The book of Amos states, *"How can two walk together unless they are agreed?" (Amos 3:3).* This shows the importance of agreement and unity in relationships, including encouraging each other to work towards achieving and maintaining these qualities.

The book of Ecclesiastes highlights the value of companionship and support in our lives. We cannot emphasize the importance of having a spouse and friend to share life's ups and downs with. This verse acknowledges that when we work together with someone, we can achieve more than we could alone. This applies to the various aspects of life, such as work, family, or personal goals. When we have someone to support us, encourage us, and provide accountability, we are more likely to succeed. (Ecclesiastes 4:9-12, KJV)

The second part of the above verse speaks to the idea that when one of us falls, we can help one another up. This could be interpreted literally as helping someone who has stumbled or fallen, and it also refers to emotional or spiritual support

44

during difficult times. When we have someone to turn to for help and guidance, we are better equipped to navigate the challenges of life.

Overall, this reminds us of the importance of relationships and communication in our lives. It encourages us to seek a meaningful connection with each other and to be willing to support and uplift one another along the way.

It is imperative to do everything in the name of the Lord Jesus and give thanks to God the Father through Him. This means that Christians should strive to live a life that honors Jesus and reflects His teachings, in both their words and actions. They should also show gratitude towards God, for all that He has provided and done for them.

Couples, this message can serve as a reminder to build your relationship on a strong foundation of faith and to seek to honor God in your relationship. We are encouraging you to act in a manner that reflects the love of God and to be grateful for each other and be a blessing in their lives. The parable in Matthew tells the story of two builders: one who builds his house on a rock and another who builds his house on sand. (Matthew, KJV)

Honoring God in a relationship can also help couples treat each other with love, kindness, and respect, as these are qualities that will strengthen your belief and religious traditions.

Showing gratitude for each other and the blessings in life can also help a couple focus on the positive aspects of their relationship and build a stronger sense of connection and appreciation for each other!

Striving to make wise choices that lead to positive outcomes requires us to be intentional in our decision-making and to consider the potential consequences of our actions.

This involves being mindful of our goals and values and taking actions that align us with our decisions. This can require patience, perseverance, and a willingness to seek advice or guidance from God when needed.

Remember, the ability to take responsibility for our decisions and strive for wise choices is an important part of personal growth and development which can lead to greater success and happiness in life.

The book of Proverbs states that the blessings that come from the Lord can lead to true richness and prosperity. That true blessings come from God, and that the blessings that He bestows upon us are not accompanied by negative consequences or sorrow.

The blessing of the LORD, it. maketh rich, and he addeth no sorrow with it. Proverbs 10:22 (KJV):

This can include blessings such as good health, financial prosperity, and fulfilling relationships. Therefore, it is important to note that this proverb does not suggest that a life of prosperity is without challenges or difficulties.

Rather, it suggests that when we receive blessings from God, we can experience true richness and abundance. These blessings can bring joy and fulfillment into our lives.

In this sense, the proverb encourages us to have faith in God and to trust in His blessings, knowing that they will ultimately lead to positive outcomes in life.

Overall, it is great that we recognize the importance of prioritizing our finances. Financial challenges can be difficult, but they can also be a valuable learning experience. It is important to assess your spending habits and make changes where necessary, such as creating and sticking to a budget, paying debts, and avoiding unnecessary expenses. Consider seeking the advice of a financial advisor or taking financial education courses to further improve your financial literacy and skills. Remember, good financial habits take time and effort to develop, but they can lead to long-term financial security and stability.

CHAPTER SIX

Geographical Location

Before the wedding day, there should be discussions and planning as to the geographical location (such as where you will live, raise a family, and place your spiritual roots) before planning the wedding and having children. Many people have different faiths and belief systems, at this stage, a spiritual counselor should not be needed. Unless there is a hard time agreeing; these decisions should be made without controversy.

It is important to have discussions and planning regarding various aspects of life, such as geographical location and getting married, and starting a family. It is important to have these conversations to ensure that both parties are on the same page and have a clear understanding of each other's expectations and goals for the future.

Spiritual counseling may not be necessary for every couple. Nevertheless, some couples may find it helpful to seek guidance from a neutral third party, especially if they have different faiths or belief systems. A spiritual counselor can help facilitate and open honest communication between individuals and assist them in finding common ground and solutions for potential conflicts.

Ultimately, the decision of whether to seek the guidance of a spiritual counselor is a personal one and should be made based on the individual needs and circumstances of each couple. The most important thing is that both parties feel they are heard and should be respected in the decision-making process.

Before marriage, one of the major decisions to consider is geographical location. Thorough research and planning should be done before deciding on a geographical location to settle down as a couple. Indeed, it is essential to consider various factors such as school systems, crime rate, taxes, employment rate, and more to ensure that you make an informed decision.

Traveling to different places that have been discussed can also provide valuable insights into the local culture, community, and way of life. It can also help you get a feel for the different neighborhoods and regions, which can help you decide where you would like to live. As a Christian couple, it is important to remember to seek guidance and protection from God as you make these decisions. Prayer and reflection can help you discern God's Will for your lives and guide you in making decisions that align with your faith and values.

It is also important to remember that the journey of marriage is not always easy, and there will be challenges along the way. Yet, with faith, commitment, and open communication, you can navigate these challenges and grow stronger together as a couple.

"Thy word is a lamp unto my feet and a light unto my path."
(Psalm 119:105, KJV)

The phrase "Thy word is a lamp unto my feet, and a light unto my path" is a verse from Psalm in the Bible. This verse is often interpreted as a metaphor for the guidance and illumination that the Word of God provides for one's life journey.

The Psalmist is expressing their trust and reliance on God's teachings and commandments to navigate the challenges and uncertainties of life. The imagery of a lamp and light suggest that God's Word illuminates the path ahead and helps the Psalmist avoid stumbling or straying from the right path.

Overall, this verse speaks to the importance of seeking guidance and wisdom from God's Word to find direction and purpose in life. It highlights the belief that God's teachings have the power to enlighten our minds, guide our decisions, and ultimately lead us to a more fulfilling and meaningful existence.

Planning should be discussed concerning where you and your family are going to live, and most of all seeking God for direction is of great importance in the decision-making process. Scripture clearly states, "The steps of a good man are ordered by the Lord: and he (God) delights in His (good man) way" (Psalms 37:23, KJV).

I thank God, my husband's family and my family were in the same city. Imagine how hard it would have been to relocate to a new environment; not knowing anyone except each other and not being familiar with the surroundings. New surroundings and new people should not worry you, if you choose to relocate let it be a consolation, *"we can do all things through Christ which strengthens us." (Philippians 4:13, KJV)*.

We are strengthened as we are consulting, seek God, and spend time with God (with our mate) we start with little strength.

It is important to seek God's guidance and direction when making important decisions, such as where to live. I acknowledge the challenges that can come with relocation to an unfamiliar environment but a reliance on God's strength and the power of faith to overcome those challenges.

Psalm 37:23 highlights the belief that God plays an active role in guiding the steps of those who seek to follow His ways. By seeking God's guidance and direction, we can be confident in the decisions of the path that God has chosen for us to take.

Philippians 4:13 emphasizes the belief that God provides the strength needed to face any challenge or obstacle that may come with relocation or other major life changes. I suggest that spending time with God and seeking His wisdom and guidance can help individuals find the strength they need to overcome any obstacle.

Overall, these passages emphasize the importance of faith and trust in God's guidance when making important life decisions, and the belief that through Him, all things are possible.

The geographic story of Abraham's relocation in Genesis 26 is a powerful example of how leaning on God's guidance can lead to blessings and success. In the passage, God instructs Abraham to leave his home and travel to a new land that God will show him. Abraham demonstrates his faith and obedience by following God's command, even though he does not know where he was going or what the future holds. Along the way, God provides for Abraham and blesses him with a large family and great wealth.

This story highlights the importance of trusting in God's guidance and following His will, even when it may require leaving behind the familiar and stepping into the unknown. It also shows how God can provide for us and bless us when we put our faith in Him and obey His commands.

We too can trust in God to provide direction and strength when making important decisions about where to live or any other major life change. By following God's guidance, we can experience the blessings that come with living in alignment with His will. Which will help couples to grow together in their faith and trust in God's plan for their lives.

This passage implies that if we solely rely on one's intellect and understanding we may not always seek the best course of action. By seeking God's wisdom and guidance, the couple can be confident in their decision to relocate and trust that God will provide the strength and resources they need to overcome any challenges they may face.

Genesis 2:24 highlights that when both partners live in the same city with their respective families, it is important to prioritize the relationship with one's spouse and leave behind any potential interference from family members. The phrase "leave and cleave" refers to the idea that when two people get married, they leave behind their families and form a new, separate unit with each other.

In practice, this means that couples must be intentional about setting boundaries and making time for each other, even if it means limiting interactions with extended family members. As the author, I am drawing from my own personal experience in suggesting that leaving family behind and prioritizing the relationship with one's spouse can help strengthen the bond between partners and promote a healthy, thriving marriage.

If both parties are committed to each other and their faith in Christ, they can weather any storms or challenges that come their way. Even still, disagreements in decision-making can create opportunities for enemies to cause discord and strife in a marriage. This underscores the importance of open communication, mutual respect, and compromise in decision-making, as well as a shared commitment to seeking God's guidance and wisdom.

I encourage all couples to prioritize their relationship with Christ and with each other in all aspects of life. By seeking unity and agreement, and guarding against division and discord, couples can build the groundwork for a thriving and fulfilling marriage.

*"All things work together for the good of them that love the
Lord and is called according to his purpose, and divine will."*
(Romans 8:28, KJV)

This emphasizes that God is sovereign and has a plan for
our lives and that even amid challenging circumstances, we
can trust in his goodness and faithfulness.

According to the word of God… *"Be sober, be vigilant;
because your adversary the devil, as a roaring lion walketh
about seeking whom he may devour:" (1 Peter 5:8, KJV)*

The imagery of a roaring lion suggests that the devil is
powerful, fierce, and intimidating, and his goal is to catch his
prey off guard and devour them. As Christians, we are called
to be sober and vigilant, that is, to be serious-minded and
alert, keeping our minds and hearts focused on God and His
ways. We must be aware of the enemy's tactics and
strategies, and resist his attempts to deceive, discourage, or
tempt us away from our faith and obedience to God.
Through prayer, reading and studying the Bible, and relying
on the power of the Holy Spirit, we can be strengthened to
withstand the enemy's attacks and overcome his schemes.

Making decisions as a couple can be challenging,
especially when the individuals involved have different
perspectives, values, and priorities. It is important to have
open and honest communication, active listening, and

mutual respect toward one another's opinions and feelings. When making decisions, it is important to consider the impact it will have on both individuals and the relationship. It may be helpful to seek the guidance of a trusted friend, or family member if you are struggling to agree. A healthy relationship requires both individuals to support the decision-making process.

Discussing and planning for geographical locations can help couples avoid potential conflicts and misunderstandings in the future. It is also important to consider factors such as job opportunities, proximity to family and friends, and the availability of a supportive community that shares your values and beliefs.

Additionally, couples should also consider their long-term goals and aspirations and how their choice of location will help them achieve these goals. These discussions and planning can help ensure that both parties are on the same page and are working towards a shared vision for their future together.

CHAPTER SEVEN

"Communication"

The book of James 1:19-20 is a wonderful place to start when encouraging people to be patient and thoughtful in their communication with others. Also, by being quick to listen, and slow to speak, we are taking the time to consider our words and respond thoughtfully instead of reacting impulsively. We are showing respect for the other person's perspective and allowing them to express themselves fully.

This advice is meant to promote effective communication and reduce conflict in relationships, especially in marriages.

In a marriage, listening is one of the most important skills that one can acquire, which can be helpful to both parties to understand each other's needs and concerns. Being quick to listen involves paying attention to what your spouse is saying, asking questions to clarify their thoughts and feelings, and showing empathy and understanding.

Being slow to speak and slow to become angry can help prevent misunderstandings and hurt feelings in marriage. By taking the time to think before responding, couples can avoid saying things they might regret later and communicate more effectively with each other.

Applying the principles in James 1:19-20 can lead to better communication and a deeper, more fulfilling relationship between spouses.

Effective communication involves both verbal and nonverbal communication, such as active listening, eye contact, and body language. It requires both parties to be willing to share their thoughts and feelings honestly and openly.

The goal of quality communication in marriage is to create a strong and healthy relationship built on mutual respect, trust and understanding. By achieving a deeper understanding of each other's needs, desires, and perspectives, couples can work together to navigate challenges, resolve conflicts, and build a shared vision for their future.

Effective communication indeed leads to several positive outcomes, including a positive response and a quick response from the recipient. When communication is effective, assumptions are minimized or eliminated, as both parties are actively seeking clarification and understanding.

Moreover, effective communication creates a neutral zone where both individuals involved are open and receptive, with their defenses down. This allows for a smoother exchange of ideas and allows for mutual understanding.

The neutral zone is a designated time and space where both partners can come together to discuss unresolved issues or situations calmly and respectfully. Setting up a neutral zone allows both spouses to approach the discussion from a place of fairness and openness, without the immediate emotional intensity that might be present right after an incident. It is often recommended to have a cool-down period before entering the neutral zone, as it allows time for emotions to settle and for both individuals to gather their thoughts.

While in the neutral zone, it is important to establish an atmosphere of mutual respect, active listening, and empathy. Each partner should have the opportunity to express their perspectives, feelings, and needs regarding the specific issue at hand. The goal is to work towards finding a resolution or compromise that satisfies both spouses.

Using the neutral zone approach can help create a safe and constructive environment for discussing sensitive topics or conflicts in a marriage. It encourages open communication, promotes understanding, and can lead to finding mutually beneficial solutions.

Remember, effective communication and compromise are key components of a healthy and successful marriage.

Verbal and non-verbal signs play a crucial role in determining the effectiveness of communication. Verbal signs such as the evidence of active listening, clear and concise speech, and appropriate tone of voice contribute to effective communication.

Non-verbal signs, including body language, facial expressions, and gestures, also provide important cues about the effectiveness of communication. When both verbal and non-verbal signs align positively, it indicates that the message has been understood and received well.

Overall, effective communication fosters understanding, reduces misunderstandings and promotes healthy relationships and collaboration between individuals. It is an essential skill that can greatly enhance personal interactions.

Asking questions to seek clarification is indeed essential to any form of communication, including within a marriage. Clarifying questions help ensure that both individuals have a clear understanding of each other's perspectives, thoughts, and feelings, and address any potential issues or conflicts before they escalate.

Showing empathy and understanding is also crucial for effective communication within a marriage. Empathy involves being able to understand and share the emotions and experiences of your spouse. It requires actively listening, acknowledging their feelings, and trying to see things from their perspective. When you demonstrate empathy, it helps create a safe and supportive environment where both parties feel heard and understood.

By practicing empathy and asking clarifying questions, you enhance the quality of communication in your marriage. These skills promote deeper understanding, strengthen the emotional connection between you and your spouse and contribute to the resolution of conflicts respectfully and constructively.

It helps to maintain a calm and respectful atmosphere where both parties can express themselves without fear of judgment or aggression.

By incorporating active listening, asking questions, showing empathy, and being patient with your words and emotions, you can improve communication in your marriage, leading to a deeper understanding, stronger emotional connection, and a healthier relationship overall.

Building a strong spiritual connection with your spouse can further enrich your relationship.

Here are some suggestions that can help you communicate effectively:

1. Self-Reflection: Take time for self-reflection and introspection. Understand your own spiritual beliefs, values, and aspirations. This self-awareness will enable you to engage in meaningful discussions and explore spiritual topics with your spouse.

2. Meaningful Conversations: Engage in open and honest conversations with your spouse about spirituality. Discuss your individual beliefs, experiences, and how your belief shaped your life. Explore deeper questions about the meaning of life, purpose, and values. These conversations can foster a sense of connection and understanding between you and your spouse.

3. Spiritual Practice: Create a spiritual practice that aligns with both your beliefs and values. This can include activities like meditation, prayer, reading spiritual texts, or engaging in traditions together. By sharing these practices, you can strengthen your spiritual bond and create a sense of unity.

4. Time of Intimacy: Intimacy goes beyond the physical aspect and can be spiritual as well. Set aside time for intimate moments where you can connect on a deeper level emotionally and spiritually. This can involve sharing dreams, aspirations, fears, and vulnerabilities.

5. The intention of the Relationship: Reflect on the primary intention of your relationship. Discuss and

understand how your spiritual journeys align and support each other. Recognize that your relationship can be a source of growth, love, and support in your spiritual paths.

By incorporating these practices into your relationship, you can foster a strong spiritual connection with your spouse. Remember that each relationship is unique, so adapt these suggestions to fit your specific beliefs, values, and circumstances.

Communication and sharing responsibilities within a household are essential for maintaining a healthy and balanced partnership. Here are some key points to consider when it comes to sharing overall household responsibilities:

1. <u>Open and Honest Communication</u>: Be open about your expectations, concerns, and preferences regarding different tasks. Effective communication ensures that both parties are aware of each other's needs and can work together to find mutually agreeable solutions.

2. <u>Identify Strengths and Interests:</u> Recognize each other's strengths, interests, and skills when allocating household responsibilities. It is often beneficial to assign tasks based on individual preferences and abilities. For example, if one party enjoys cooking while the other prefers cleaning, you can divide those responsibilities accordingly.

3.   Create a Shared Vision: Discuss and establish a shared vision for your household. Talk about your long-term goals, financial plans, and priorities. This shared vision helps guide your decision-making process and ensures that both parties are working towards common goals.

4.   Fair Division of Responsibilities: Aim for an equitable distribution of household responsibilities. It may not always mean a perfectly equal split, as each partnership is unique, and roles may vary based on individual circumstances. But strive for a division that feels fair and balanced to both parties. Regularly reassess and adjust as needed.

5.   Flexibility   and   Adaptability: Household responsibilities can change over time due to various factors like work demands, family dynamics, or personal circumstances. Be flexible and willing to adapt the division of tasks to accommodate these changes. Regularly check in with each other and make necessary adjustments to ensure a sustainable and harmonious balance.

6.   Appreciation and Support: Recognize and appreciate each   other's   efforts   in   managing   household responsibilities. Express gratitude for the tasks performed by your spouse and provide support when needed.

Encouragement and acknowledgment go a long way in fostering a positive and collaborative environment.

Remember, the key is to approach household responsibilities as a shared endeavor, where both parties contribute and support each other. By communicating openly, respecting each other's strengths, and maintaining a flexible and supportive mindset, you can establish a balanced and harmonious division of responsibilities within your household.

When it comes to financial matters, communicating about the family budget is crucial. Financial disagreements can often lead to stress and strain in a relationship.

Here are some important topics to consider:

1. <u>Set Shared Financial Goals</u>: Discuss and establish shared financial goals as a couple. This may include saving for specific milestones, creating an emergency fund, or planning for future expenses. By having common objectives, both parties can work together towards achieving them.

2. <u>Regular Budget Discussions</u>: Schedule regular budget discussions to review your income, expenses, and savings. This allows you to track your financial progress, identify areas where adjustments can be made, and ensures that you are staying on track with your financial goals.

3.   Be Transparent About Income and Expenses: Both parties should be open and transparent about their income, debts, and individual expenses. This helps create a clear picture of your financial situation and enables informed decision-making.

4.   Collaborative Decision-Making: Involve both parties in the financial decision-making process. Major expenses should be discussed and agreed upon together. This ensures that both individuals have a say in how money is being spent and helps prevent potential conflicts or feelings of resentment.

5.   Budget for Individual Needs: Allow room in the budget for personal discretionary spending. Each party should have some financial autonomy for personal interests and hobbies. Establishing individual allowances within the budget can help maintain a sense of independence and fairness.

6.   Emergency Planning: Discuss and plan for unforeseen circumstances and emergencies. Set aside funds in your budget for emergencies, such as medical expenses or unexpected home repairs. Being prepared for unexpected financial situations can help reduce stress and uncertainty.

7.   Seek Professional Advice if Needed: If you find it challenging to manage your finances as a couple, consider seeking the guidance of a financial advisor or counselor.

They can provide expert advice and help you create a financial plan that suits your unique circumstances.

Remember, open and honest communication about finances is crucial to building trust, avoiding financial conflicts, and achieving your shared goals. Regularly discussing the family budget, making joint decisions, and being mindful of your spending contributes to a healthier financial foundation for your marriage.

Open and honest communication about your feelings is vitally important in any marriage, especially in the early stages. It is important to express your thoughts, emotions, and concerns with your spouse rather than keeping them hidden.

Here are some reasons why open communication about feelings is beneficial:

1. Emotional Connection: Sharing your feelings with your spouse strengthens the emotional bond you share. When you express your emotions, it allows your spouse to understand you on a deeper level and nurtures a sense of intimacy and connection.

2. Problem Resolution: Communicating your feelings helps address any underlying issues or conflicts in your marriage. By expressing your concerns or frustrations,

you create an opportunity to work together towards finding resolutions and making necessary adjustments.

3. Validation and Support: Sharing your feelings allows your spouse to validate and support you. It helps them understand your perspective, offer empathy, and provide the emotional support you may need. This creates a safe environment where both parties can feel heard and valued.

4. Prevention of Resentment: When feelings are left unexpressed, they can build up over time and lead to resentment. By communicating your emotions early on, you can prevent these feelings from festering and address them in a timely manner.

5. Building Trust: Openly expressing your feelings builds trust in your marriage. It shows that you are willing to be vulnerable and that you value honesty and authenticity. Trust is essential for a strong and healthy relationship.

6. Enhancing Understanding: Sharing your feelings helps both parties to understand triggers, needs, and boundaries. It provides them with insights into your emotional landscape and helps them navigate the relationship with greater empathy and sensitivity.

Remember, effective communication involves both parties expressing their feelings and actively listening to one another. Creating a safe and non-judgmental space for open dialogue encourages a healthy and supportive atmosphere in a marriage.

Discussing outside friendships is important in the early stages of a marriage as well. Openly discussing and understanding each other's friendships can help establish boundaries, prevent misunderstandings, and maintain a healthy balance between individual friendships and marriage itself.

Here are some points to consider:

1.   Open and Honest Communication: Have open and honest conversations about your friendships and encourage your spouse to do the same. Discuss the nature of your friendships, the frequency of interactions, and any potential concerns or boundaries you may have.

2.   Mutual Understanding: Seek to understand each other's perspectives and values regarding friendships. Recognize that friendships play an important role in a person's life, but also understand that your primary commitment is to your marriage.

3.   Establishing Boundaries: Establish clear boundaries, as a couple, that both parties feel comfortable with. This

may include discussing expectations around spending time with friends, maintaining individual friendships, and addressing potential situations that could create tension in the marriage.

4.   Trust and Respect: It is important to trust each other's judgment and intentions when it comes to friendships. Respect each other's need for social connections and maintain transparency and honesty about interactions with friends.

5.   Regular Check-Ins: Periodically check in with each other to ensure that both parties feel comfortable and secure with the friendships involved. If concerns or issues arise, address them openly and calmly, seeking resolutions that work for both of you.

Remember, healthy marriages involve a balance between individuality and togetherness. Supporting each other's friendships and maintaining open communication about them can contribute to a strong and trusting relationship.

By openly discussing and understanding each other's friendships from the beginning, you can prevent potential problems and establish a high standard of mutual respect and trust.

While maintaining open and honest communication is essential in a marriage, it is also important to find a balance to avoid overwhelming each other. It is healthy to keep in mind that certain aspects of marriage, such as traveling alone or making decisions without your spouse, should be approached with consideration and respect for the relationship.

Here are some points to consider:

1. Open Dialogue: Discuss situations like solo travel or decision-making processes to ensure both partners feel heard and understood.

2. Mutual Trust: Build and maintain trust by being transparent, reliable, and supportive of each other's independence.

3. Mutual Respect: Respect for each other's autonomy is key. While marriage involves partnership, it is also important to recognize and respect individuality. Each party should have the freedom to pursue personal interests, make decisions, and engage in solo activities if it does not compromise the well-being and trust within the relationship.

4. Consideration and Inclusion: When making decisions or planning activities, consider the impact on your spouse. Communicate and involve your spouse in the discussions when appropriate, especially for

significant decisions that may affect both of you and your shared resources.

5. Balancing Independence and Togetherness: Find a balance between cultivating individuality and maintaining a sense of togetherness. Recognize that personal autonomy can contribute positively to the relationship, but also ensure that you prioritize and nurture your connection as a couple.

Remember, every couple is unique, and what works for one may not work for another. It is important to have ongoing conversations with your spouse about your expectations, boundaries, and comfort levels regarding solo activities and decision-making. By maintaining open and respectful communication, you can strengthen your relationship.

A strong bond can provide a sense of security, trust, and emotional connection. These are vital for a successful marriage. It is important to continue nurturing and strengthening that bond throughout your marriage through open communication, mutual respect, and shared experiences. Celebrate the growth and strength of your relationship, so that it may continue to flourish in the years to come.

"So, they are no longer two, but one flesh. Therefore, what God has joined together, let no one separate" (Matthew 19:6).

CHAPTER EIGHT

"Sacrifices"

Sacrifices can indeed be meaningful and impactful when approached with the right mindset and purpose. While the concept of sacrifice typically involves giving up something of value, it can lead to personal growth, achievements, and positive outcomes. When you positively embrace sacrifice, it often signifies your dedication, commitment, and willingness to prioritize something important over immediate gratification or comfort. It can reflect your determination to achieve long-term goals, support others, or contribute to a greater cause.

By recognizing the value and purpose behind your sacrifices, you can find a sense of fulfillment, personal satisfaction, and even happiness. It can strengthen your character, resilience, and discipline. Sacrifices can also foster empathy, compassion, and gratitude as you realize the efforts and contributions of others.

It is crucial to strike a balance *and* ensure that your sacrifices align with your values, well-being, and the well-being of those around you. It is essential to consider the potential consequences and evaluate whether the sacrifices you make are sustainable, healthy, and aligned with your overall goals and values.

The meaning and impact of sacrifices are subjective and vary depending on individual circumstances and perspectives. It is important to reflect on your choices, find purpose in your sacrifices, and ensure they contribute positively to your life and the lives of others. Sacrifice is often a significant aspect of a marriage or any committed partnership. It involves both individuals willingly giving up certain personal desires, preferences or needs for the sake of the relationship's well-being and growth.

In marriage, sacrifice can take many forms. It could mean compromising on decisions, prioritizing the needs and happiness of your spouse, adjusting to accommodate each other's goals and aspirations, or providing emotional support during challenging times.

These sacrifices can strengthen the bond between you and your spouse to create a foundation of love, trust, and mutual understanding.

The key element in navigating sacrifices within a marriage is the presence of love. When sacrifices are made with genuine love and care for one another, they become more meaningful and sustainable. It is crucial to approach sacrifices as an act of selflessness and a demonstration of your commitment to the relationship.

It is vitally important to be open and honest in your communication while trying to understand each other's needs and expectations. It allows you to find a balance between individual desires and the collective well-being of the marriage. Both parties should actively listen, express their feelings, and seek compromising solutions that honor the needs and happiness of both individuals.

While sacrifices are an essential part of marriage, it is also important to ensure that neither party feels consistently burdened or neglected. Maintaining a healthy balance between personal fulfillment and sacrifices for the relationship is crucial. It requires ongoing effort, understanding, and the willingness to adapt as an individual and as a couple. Remember, sacrifices in a marriage should be a two-way street, with both parties contributing and supporting each other.

When sacrifices are reciprocated and appreciated, they can deepen the connection and create a strong foundation for fulfillment and love. Choosing a direction in life, including decisions about attending a particular church, can indeed be significant for an individual.

It is important to have personal beliefs, values, and convictions, and sometimes these may differ from those of your spouse. While it is crucial to respect and consider each other's perspectives, finding a way to navigate through such differences is important for maintaining a healthy and harmonious relationship.

Here are a few considerations when facing differing views on attending a particular church or any other life choices within a marriage:

1.   Have respectful communication: Engage in honest and respectful conversations with your spouse about your beliefs, values, and the reasons behind your preferences. Seek to understand each other's perspectives without judgment or criticism.

2.   Active listener with empathy: Truly listen to your spouse's thoughts, emotions, and concerns. Empathize with their point of view, even if you may disagree. Showing understanding and empathy can foster a sense of trust and openness within the relationship.

3.   Having common ground: Explore areas of agreement and shared values. Focus on the aspects that you both find important and that align with your shared goals and

aspirations. Look for compromises or solutions that can honor both perspectives.

4. <u>Respect individual autonomy:</u> Recognize that individuals have the right to make choices that align with their own beliefs and convictions. Respect your spouse's autonomy and their right to choose their own spiritual path or life direction.

5. <u>Find a middle ground:</u> Explore options where you can find a balance between your differing views. This could involve attending different churches on alternating weeks, participating in activities that fulfill your individual spiritual needs, or finding other ways to nourish your spiritual needs while maintaining a sense of togetherness.

6. <u>Seek support:</u> If the differences become challenging to navigate on your own, consider seeking guidance from a trusted counselor, religious leader, or marriage therapist. They can provide insights and strategies to help you navigate these differences effectively.

Remember, every relationship is unique, and what works for one couple may not work for another. The most important aspect is to approach these differences with love, respect, and open-mindedness, keeping the overall well-being and happiness of both parties at the forefront.

Entering a marriage is indeed a significant decision that often involves sacrifices and a level of uncertainty about the future. Marriage requires a deep commitment, emotional investment, and a willingness to navigate the challenges and uncertainties that may arise.

When two individuals decide to marry, they make a conscious choice to embark on a lifelong journey together, despite not knowing precisely what lies ahead.

This decision entails sacrificing certain aspects of individual autonomy, adapting to the needs and desires of both parties, and committing to working through the ups and downs that may come their way.

Here are a few points to consider regarding the sacrifice and uncertainty involved in entering a marriage:

1.   Trust and faith: A strong foundation of trust and faith in each other is vital when entering a marriage. Trusting that you and your spouse share similar values, commitment, and dedication to the relationship can provide a sense of security even in the face of uncertainty.

2.   Emotional investment: Marriage requires emotional vulnerability and investment. It means opening oneself up to the possibility of both joy and pain, knowing that challenges and uncertainties may arise. The willingness to invest emotionally is a sacrifice that contributes to the growth and strength of the relationship.

3. Shared responsibility: In a marriage, both parties share the responsibility of navigating the unknown future together. It involves making joint decisions, supporting each other's dreams and aspirations, and working together as a team to overcome challenges and uncertainties.

4. Growth and adaptation: Marriage often requires personal growth and adaptation as an individual and as a couple. It may involve sacrificing certain individual desires or adjusting expectations to accommodate the needs of the relationship. Flexibility and a willingness to adapt are crucial when facing the uncertainties that come with marriage.

5. Commitment and perseverance: The commitment to stay dedicated to marriage, even in uncertain times, is a sacrifice. It means persevering through difficult moments, seeking resolution and compromise, and continually nurturing the relationship.

While entering a marriage does involve sacrifices and uncertainties, it also offers the opportunity for love, companionship, growth, and fulfillment. It is a journey that, when approached with open hearts, commitment, and a willingness to face the unknown together, can lead to a deep and meaningful connection between each other.

When it comes to altering roles, schedules, and finances within a marriage, it often requires sacrifices and reflects the commitment within the union. As life evolves and circumstances change, couples may need to adjust their roles, redistribute responsibilities, adapt their schedules, and make financial decisions that impact both parties. These changes can require sacrifices from both individuals and demonstrate their commitment to the relationship.

Here are some key aspects to consider regarding the sacrifices and commitment involved in altering roles, schedules, and finances in a marriage:

1. <u>Flexibility and adaptability:</u> Being open to altering roles, schedules, and finances requires flexibility and adaptability from both parties. It involves recognizing the need for change and being willing to adjust accordingly to support each other and the overall well-being of the marriage.

2. <u>Communication and collaboration:</u> Effective communication is crucial when discussing and making decisions about roles, schedules, and finances. Engage in open and honest conversations, express your needs and concerns, and actively listen to your spouse's perspective. Collaboration and mutual decision-making ensure that sacrifices are shared and that both parties have a voice in shaping the changes.

3. <u>Mutual support and understanding:</u> Altering roles, schedules, and finances often means that one or both

parties will need to make sacrifices. It is important to provide support and understanding during these transitions. Recognize that sacrifices made by one party may benefit the overall stability and happiness of the marriage.

4. Shared responsibility: When altering roles and finances, it is essential to have a shared understanding of the responsibilities involved. Both parties should contribute to decision-making and actively participate in the new arrangements. This shared responsibility reinforces the commitment to working together as a team.

5. Financial transparency and planning: Financial decisions are a crucial aspect of altering finances within a marriage. Open and honest discussions about financial goals, budgets, and long-term plans are essential. Both parties should have a clear understanding of the financial situation and actively contribute to the planning process.

6. Mutual growth and fulfillment: While sacrifices may be necessary, it is important to ensure that both parties have opportunities for personal growth and fulfillment within the altered roles, schedules, and finances. Strive to find a balance that supports individual aspirations and the collective well-being of the marriage.

While the sacrifices and commitment required to alter roles, schedules, and finances in a marriage demonstrate a willingness to adapt and prioritize the needs of the relationship. By approaching these changes with open communication, understanding, and collaboration, couples can navigate them together and strengthen their commitment and bond. This sentiment reflects a powerful commitment to the strength and unity of your union.

As a couple you vowed to stand together through both wealth and financial challenges, which is an acknowledgment that the bond you share transcends material circumstances.

It emphasizes the resilience and dedication required to navigate life's ups and downs as a team. When couples make a promise to stay united through richer or poorer, they affirm their commitment to supporting each other in various financial situations. This commitment goes beyond mere monetary wealth and encompasses emotional support, shared decision-making, and a willingness to adapt and find solutions together.

Here are a few key elements that contribute to maintaining unity in the face of financial circumstances:

1. Open communication: Transparent and honest communication about financial matters is crucial. Discuss financial goals, concerns, and plans openly, ensuring that both parties have a clear understanding of the overall financial picture.

2.   Shared fiscal responsibility: Collaborate on financial decisions and actively participate in managing finances as a team. This approach promotes a sense of unity and mutual ownership, reducing the potential for financial strain to create division within the relationship.

3.   Budgeting and financial planning: Create a budget and financial plan that aligns with your shared goals and values. This can help maintain financial stability and reduce stress. Regularly review and adjust your plan as needed, considering any changes in income or expenses.

4.   Support and understanding: Show empathy and support during challenging financial times. Recognize that financial struggles can be stressful and emotionally taxing. By providing emotional support, you can strengthen your bond and face difficulties together.

5.   Adaptability and resourcefulness: Cultivate a mindset of adaptability and resourcefulness. Explore creative solutions, seek opportunities for growth and development, and be open to adjusting your lifestyle or pursuing new avenues for financial stability.

6.   Focus on non-material aspects: Remind yourselves of the non-material aspects that enrich your relationship, such as shared values, love, trust, and companionship. By nurturing these elements, you can reinforce the foundation of your union beyond financial circumstances.

Remember that every couple's financial journey is unique, and challenges may arise along the way. By embracing the commitment to stand together for richer or poorer, you demonstrate a deep understanding of the true essence of your union and a willingness to support each other unconditionally.

Building trust as a new couple is a vital aspect of a strong and healthy relationship. Sacrifice can play a role in fostering trust between partners by demonstrating commitment, reliability, and selflessness.

Here are some suggestions on how you can gain trust through sacrifice:

1. Open and honest communication: Establish a foundation of open and honest communication. Share your thoughts, feelings, and expectations with each other. Discuss your boundaries, needs, and desires, ensuring that you both have a clear understanding of what trust means to each of you.

2. Follow through on commitments: Make promises or commitments that you are genuinely willing to keep. When you make sacrifices for each other, follow through on them consistently. Reliability and consistency in your actions will help build trust over time.

3.   Support each other's goals: Show genuine support for each other's individual goals and aspirations. Make sacrifices to help your partner pursue their dreams, even if it means temporarily setting aside some of your own desires. By demonstrating selflessness and being actively supportive, you can build trust and foster a sense of unity.

4.   Share responsibilities and make joint decisions: Distribute responsibilities and decision-making equally, based on your strengths and interests. Make sacrifices to accommodate each other's needs and ensure that both partners have a say in the relationship. This balance of power and shared decision-making promotes trust and equality.

5.   Be reliable in small matters: Trust is built through consistency in both big and small matters. Show reliability and dependability in everyday situations, such as being punctual, keeping your promises, and being there for each other during times of need. These small acts of sacrifice and reliability accumulate over time and contribute to trust-building.

6.   Be vulnerable and empathetic: Allow yourselves to be vulnerable with each other. Share your fears, insecurities, and vulnerabilities, and provide a safe space for your partner to do the same. Demonstrate empathy and

understanding when your partner makes sacrifices for you and reciprocate by offering support and validation.

7.   Patience and forgiveness: Building trust takes time and effort. Be patient with each other's growth and forgive mistakes along the way. Understand that sacrifices and trust-building are ongoing processes, and it is normal to encounter setbacks or challenges. Work through them together with compassion and forgiveness.

Remember, trust is nurtured through consistent actions, open communication, and mutual support. By making sacrifices that prioritize the well-being of your partner and the relationship, you can lay a strong foundation of trust that will contribute to the growth and longevity of your bond.

In writing this chapter on sacrifice, trust, and relationships, this context was a meaningful undertaking during the first stages of our marriage. In fact, sacrifice and trust go hand in hand, and their combination has been essential to the development and strengthening of our relationship.

Making sacrifices for each other in marriage shows our determination and willingness to prioritize each other's well-being before our own. These sacrifices can be both material and immaterial, such as giving up personal desires, compromising decisions, and investing time and effort in furthering the goals of others.

Through these sacrificial acts, trust begins to grow. Here is how making sacrifices can help build trust in our relationships.

A. <u>Vulnerability and Selflessness:</u> Sacrifice requires vulnerability and selflessness. By being understanding, we show each other that we trust each other enough to reveal our needs, desires, and weaknesses. Our willingness to put their well-being first shows our selflessness and creates a foundation of trust.

B. <u>Reliability and Consistency</u>: A pattern of reliability and consistency emerges when you consistently make sacrifices for your spouse. That way, you can trust them to keep their promises and expect support when needed. This reliability makes them aware that you are there for them, even if it requires a personal sacrifice, and builds trust.

C. <u>Mutual understanding of empathy</u>: Relationships are often born out of understanding and empathy. Making sacrifices for your spouse shows that you truly understand their needs and wants. This understanding deepens the emotional connection and builds trust.

D. <u>Increased engagement:</u> Making sacrifices is a testament to your commitment to your relationship. This shows that you are willing to act for the benefit of others over your own and strengthens your resolve to get married.

E. <u>Reciprocity and Mutual Support:</u> Sacrifice gives both sides creative talents with a commitment to reciprocity and mutual support. Exchanging sacrifices creates a give-and-take within the relationship. This mutual support builds trust as each individual feels valued in the relationship.

In summary, making sacrifices for each other builds trust in a marriage. Sacrifice requires vulnerability, selflessness, reliability, empathy, devotion, and mutual support. As you navigate through the first stages of your marriage and explore the depths of sacrifice, you will find that trust naturally grows, creating a strong and resilient bond between you and your partner.

CHAPTER NINE

"Faith, Marriage, and Family"

Prioritizing Self Before Parenthood: A Path to Personal Fulfillment

In this chapter, we will delve into the significance of prioritizing our own lives before incorporating the responsibility of raising children. We know that becoming a parent is a life-changing experience that brings immense joy and fulfillment, it is essential to recognize the importance of self-care, personal growth, and individual goals before embarking on the journey of parenthood.

By prioritizing ourselves first, we can establish a solid foundation for our own happiness and well-being, ultimately benefiting both ourselves and our future children.

1. Nurturing Personal Growth:

a. Self-Exploration: Taking the time to understand our own values, interests, and aspirations can help us develop a strong sense of self. This self-awareness is crucial in creating a fulfilling life and setting an example for our children.

b. Pursuing Passions: Prioritizing our hobbies, interests, and career goals allows us to cultivate our talents and find personal fulfillment. By nurturing our passions, we model a life of purpose and dedication for our children to emulate.

2. Mental and Emotional Well-Being:

a. Self-Care: Investing in our own physical, mental, and emotional well-being is essential for maintaining a healthy and balanced life. Prioritizing self-care activities such as exercise, relaxation, and seeking support when needed enables us to be better equipped to handle the challenges of parenthood.

b. Emotional Resilience: Building emotional resilience through self-reflection, therapy, or other personal growth practices prepares us to navigate the inevitable ups and downs of parenting, ensuring we can provide a stable and nurturing environment for our children.

3. Establishing Stronger Relationships:

a. Partner or Spousal Connection: Prioritizing your relationship with your spouse before having children strengthens the foundation of your family unit. Maintaining open communication, fostering intimacy, and nurturing the bond between couples, can contribute to a harmonious parenting journey.

b. Supportive Network: A relationship with your friends, family, and a support network is crucial for parental well-being. Fostering these connections before becoming a parent will establish a robust support system that can offer guidance and assistance when needed.

4. Financial Stability:

a. Achieving Financial Goals: Financial stability by setting goals, managing debt, and building savings, provides a secure foundation before starting a family. Having a solid financial plan in place will allow you to provide for your children's needs and offer them a stable upbringing.

Conclusion: Incorporating children into your lives is a significant and rewarding step, but it is crucial to prioritize your own well-being and personal growth before taking on the responsibilities of parenthood.

Investing in oneself, nurturing your passions, and establishing a solid foundation in various aspects of your life, can create a nurturing and fulfilling environment for both you and your future children. Remember, taking care of ourselves first is not selfish but rather an act of love that benefits everyone that is involved.

Indeed, faith, marriage, and family are significant aspects of many people's lives. Faith can provide a sense of purpose, guidance, and fulfillment. It often serves as a source of strength and support for individuals who are seeking to find meaning and wholeness in their lives.

The context of faith that many people experience is a profound sense of connection with something greater than themselves. This connection often helps to fill a void or emptiness that may exist within their hearts and souls. By embracing their faith, individuals can find comfort, hope, and a deeper understanding of their purpose in life, which can enhance a relationship.

Marriage and family will also bring a wonderful element, which brings joy, companionship, and a sense of belonging to many individuals. These relationships provide a foundation of love, support, and shared experiences that contribute to personal growth and emotional well-being. The commitment and dedication involved in a marriage and the bond within a family can be deeply fulfilling and enriching.

It is important to note that faith and biblical principles can be invaluable to many individuals and families; personal interpretations and practices may vary. Each person's understanding and application of their faith and the Bible may differ, and it is essential to respect diverse perspectives within the context of religious beliefs and practices.

Relying on one's faith and biblical principles can provide a stronger foundation and guidance in navigating various aspects of life, including relationships and family dynamics. The Bible offers wisdom, moral teachings, and principles that many individuals find comforting and applicable to their daily lives.

As a Christian, the Bible serves as a source of inspiration and direction in making decisions, resolving conflicts, and nurturing relationships within the family unit. It can provide guidance on topics such as love, forgiveness, communication, respect, and the importance of unity and mutual support.

Individuals often strive to create a harmonious and loving environment within the family union by applying biblical principles. By looking towards the scriptures for guidance on parenting, resolving conflicts, showing compassion, and fostering spiritual growth within the household.

Faith in a higher power can bring a sense of peace, hope, and resilience during challenging times within a family. Believers may find comfort in prayer, seeking solace and strength from their faith community, and trusting in the divine plan for their lives.

Everyone's faith and beliefs are shaped by their personal experiences, upbringing, culture, and various other factors. While everyone's journey and experiences may be unique, we can still share and discuss our experiences with others as a means of understanding and learning from different perspectives.

Sharing our experiences can be a valuable method for fostering understanding, empathy, and dialogue among individuals with different beliefs. It allows us to gain insight into the diverse ways people interpret and experience their faith or spirituality. By listening and sharing experiences, we can broaden our understanding, challenge our preconceptions, and build bridges of communication and respect.

It is important to approach these discussions with an open mind, respect for differing viewpoints, and a willingness to learn from others. While we may not always agree with or fully understand someone else's experiences, engaging in thoughtful and respectful dialogue can help promote tolerance, mutual understanding, and a more inclusive society.

Sharing your biblical experiences within your marriage can be a meaningful way to offer guidance and support to other couples who may be facing similar challenges or seeking spiritual guidance in their relationships. By sharing your experiences, you can provide practical insights, lessons learned, and biblical principles that have helped you navigate your marriage.

When sharing your experiences, it can be helpful to consider a few key points:

1. Context: Provides relevant background information about your relationship and the specific situations or challenges you have encountered. This helps others understand the context of your experiences.

2. Lessons Learned: Reflect on the lessons you have learned from sharing biblical experiences and how they have impacted your marriage. Share practical advice and actionable steps that others can apply to their relationships.

3. Biblical Foundation: Highlight the biblical principles and teachings that have influenced your perspective and

decisions within the marriage. Share how these principles have shaped your understanding and actions, and how they can be applied to other couples.

4. Respect Individual Differences: Recognize that every marriage is unique, and what worked for us may not necessarily work for others. Encourage couples to seek God's guidance in their relationships and to adapt the lessons to their specific circumstances.

5. Encourage Dialogue: Invite couples to engage in open and honest conversations with each other and with God. Emphasize the importance of communication, forgiveness, and mutual respect in building a strong and healthy marriage.

Remember, while your experiences can offer valuable insights, it is important to acknowledge that every relationship is different, and there is no one-size-fits-all solution. Encourage couples to seek professional counseling or guidance from their spiritual leaders when needed.

The term "**discovery zone**" used in the context of marriage and family, refers to the idea that these areas of life, provide an opportunity for exploration, growth, and self-discovery. Let us break down why it is called the discovery zone:

1. <u>Exploration</u>: Faith, marriage, and family offer individuals a chance to explore their beliefs, values, and personal growth. It is a time when individuals may delve deeper into their faith, understand their roles and responsibilities within a marriage, and navigate the dynamics of family relationships.

2. <u>Growth</u>: Engaging in faith, marriage, and family life often leads to personal growth. It involves learning, adapting, and evolving as individuals navigate the challenges and joys that come with these areas. Through experiences and interactions, individuals have opportunities for personal development, emotional maturity, and spiritual growth.

3. <u>Self-Discovery</u>: Faith, marriage, and family can be transformative, leading individuals to discover more about themselves. They provide a platform for self-reflection, understanding one's strengths and weaknesses, and uncovering aspects of their identity and purpose.

4. <u>Settling within the Union</u>: The phrase "takes our rightful place" suggests the process of finding one's role and purpose within the context of faith, marriage, and family. It involves understanding and embracing the responsibilities and commitments associated with these areas and finding a sense of belonging and fulfillment within them.

The discovery zone reflects the notion that faith, marriage, and family are dynamic discoveries where individuals can explore, grow, and understand themselves, their spouse, and their place in the union. It is a continuous journey of self-discovery and finding meaning in these important aspects of life.

These areas of a union should be fitly joined together for all to partake in, as it is the will of God, which reflects the understanding that faith, marriage, and family are interconnected and integral aspects of life.

From a religious perspective, the concept of the will of God encompasses the belief that God has a purpose and a plan for individuals and their relationships. (Jeremiah 29:11) This includes the institution of marriage and the importance of family. When individuals align their lives with God's Will, they can experience greater fulfillment, joy, and blessings in their faith, marriage, and family life.

By acknowledging and actively participating in these areas, individuals live in accordance with God's design and teachings. This can involve practicing and sharing values, nurturing relationships based on love and mutual respect, and seeking spiritual growth within the context of the family unit.

Furthermore, the notion of all individuals partaking in these areas suggests inclusiveness and the belief that faith, marriage, and family are meant to be shared experiences. It highlights the importance of communal support, accountability, and the understanding that these aspects of life are not solely individual pursuits, but rather collective endeavors.

It is important to note that interpretations of God's will and the understanding of how faith, marriage, and family are joined together may vary among different religious traditions and individual beliefs. It is a deeply personal and spiritual matter, and individuals may have different perspectives on how these aspects of life intersect and are guided by their faith.

Therefore, what God has joined together, let no one separate.
(Mark 10:9)

In sharing the duties, a husband is to provide support for his wife, to protect her from danger, and to cherish her with unwavering affection. Their belief should be rooted in the commands of God's Word, which ordains the husband's responsibility for the provision and support of his wife.

It is important to take into consideration that gender roles and marital responsibilities can vary based on cultural, religious, and personal beliefs. Different interpretations of religious texts and cultural norms can influence people's perspectives on these matters.

In some religious and cultural backgrounds, there are teachings and beliefs that outline specific roles and responsibilities within the marriage. These beliefs can be assigned according to traditional gender roles, including the husband as the primary provider and protector of the family, while the wife may be seen as primarily responsible for domestic duties and caregiving for the family.

It is essential to recognize that societal norms and understandings of gender roles have evolved over time, and there is no singular or universally accepted interpretation of these roles. Many couples today strive for equal partnership and shared responsibilities within their marriages, where both partners contribute to the support and well-being of the family unit in various ways.

The dynamics of marriage and the roles and responsibilities within it should be based on the mutual understanding, agreement, and preferences of the individuals involved. It is important for couples to communicate openly, respect each other's desires and abilities, and find a balance that works for their specific relationship and circumstances. The wife is to respect and support her husband. The husband is to respect and support his wife. (1 Peter 3:4; Mark 10:7)

In various religious and cultural traditions, there are teachings and interpretations that emphasize the importance of mutual respect, support, and unity within a marriage. These teachings often emphasize the significance of love, commitment, and the establishment of a strong bond between husband and wife.

The concept of a wife adorning herself with a meek and quiet spirit is rooted in biblical teachings and is understood by some to signify humility, gentleness, and a calm demeanor. It is often seen as a characteristic that promotes harmony and fosters a peaceful atmosphere within the marriage.

Mark 10:7 highlights the idea that when a man and woman enter marriage, they form a new family unit that is separate from their respective parents. It signifies the unity and commitment between husband and wife, symbolizing the merging of their lives and responsibilities.

It is important for couples to engage in open and respectful communication, understanding, and cooperation to create a healthy and balanced marital relationship that aligns with their shared values and beliefs.

Referencing the discovery zone, the Bible states, "The husband is the head of the wife, even as Christ is the head of the church: and He is the savior of the whole body, that He

(Christ) might sanctify and cleanse it with the washing of water by the word, that he might present it to himself a glorious church. No man ever yet hated his own flesh; but nourishes and cherish it even as the Lord loves the church: we are members of His (Christ's) body; of His flesh, of His bones." (Ephesians 5:23, 26-27NKJV)

Some of the areas of concern engaged in by young couples is what we (my husband and I) call "Union duties stress." Union duties stress consists of couples assigning each other duties as opposed to doing everything equally.

"My husband and I worked together sharing the duties until all the duties were completed."

Unfortunately, some couples feel as though it is a 'man's' job to take out the trash and a 'woman's' job to cook and clean. Couples should enter their marriage with an open mind without assigning a task to a specific gender, some couples go as far as having separate checking accounts and splitting the rent and bills, etc.

Please understand! Couples are not roommates. Union duties instead of working together as one can cause stress in the relationship. Union duties stress is an area young couples, or couples, in general, should not allow the enemy to cause them to be tempted, the bible states:

"The enemy (thief) comes to steal, and to kill, and to destroy I am come that they might have life, and that they might have it more abundantly." (John 10:10KJV)

However, through our faith, we can focus on the biblical principles of family and marriage. When entering a union, such as a marriage, it is important to prioritize various aspects of your life. While faith, marriage, and family can be significant aspects for many people, the order of priority may vary depending on individual beliefs and values.

Here is a perspective on prioritizing these elements:

1. Personal Values: It is crucial to start by identifying your values and beliefs. Reflect on what matters most to you and how you want to shape your life. This self-reflection will help you establish a foundation for your priorities.

2. Faith: For individuals who have religious or spiritual beliefs, faith can play a central role in their lives. It provides a framework for understanding the world, guides decision-making, and can be a source of strength and support. If faith is a fundamental aspect of your life, it is reasonable to prioritize nurturing and living according to your spiritual values.

3. Marriage: Once you have committed to a marriage, it is essential to prioritize the well-being and growth of the relationship. This involves investing time, effort, and

emotional energy into building a strong and healthy partnership. Effective communication, mutual respect, trust, and shared goals are crucial elements to prioritize in a marriage.

4. <u>Family:</u> If you and your spouse choose to have or already have children, the well-being and nurturing of the family unit become important priorities. This includes creating a loving and supportive environment, providing for the physical and emotional needs, and actively participating in your growth and development. It is essential to strike a balance between individual needs, marital needs, and the needs of the family.

It is worth mentioning that priorities can shift and evolve over time as circumstances change and new challenges arise. Flexibility, open communication, and adaptability are key to finding the right balance between faith, marriage, family, and other aspects of life such as personal growth, career, and community involvement.

In conclusion, it is important to define your priorities based on your values, beliefs, and the needs of your specific situation.

CHAPTER TEN

Until Death, Do We Part

The Scriptures have always demonstrated that 'God Ordains Marriages':

Genesis 2:18-25; Malachi 2:13-16; Matthew 19;3-12

Colossians 3:18-4:1

From the beginning of time, God has demonstrated his love through the bride and groom for marriage! Marriage is indeed a concept that has been present throughout history of all time. It is true that some religious beliefs and traditional marriages are sacred unions that symbolize love and the relationship between God and humanity. The bride and groom are often used to illustrate this spiritual connection.

GOD ORDAINS MARRIAGES

The relationship between Christ and the Church is often metaphorically described as the bridegroom and bride. This symbolism highlights the love, commitment, and sacrificial nature of Christ's relationship with His followers. Marriage is seen as a reflection of His divine love, where the husband and wife are called to love, honor, and support each other.

Different individuals and societies may prioritize marriage for various reasons, and the importance of faith, love, commitment, and family may differ among individuals based on their personal beliefs and values. It is crucial to respect diverse perspectives and understand the interpretations of marriage.

Though, it is equally important that you try and remember divine order. Divine order refers to the belief that there is a higher plan or purpose set by a higher power, such as God, and that adhering to this order leads to a more fulfilling and meaningful life.

Let us reconsider and revisit these promises; you will understand why traditional marriage vows have endured. Making these vows before God and keeping them is deeply meaningful and is worth any effort involved.

The phrase 'till death do us part' is indeed a common component of traditional marriage vows and signifies a lifelong commitment to one's spouse. The reference I mentioned from Matthew 19:4-6 highlights the biblical perspective on marriage and emphasizes the sacred nature of the marital bond.

In this passage, Jesus affirms the creation of male and female and quotes the words from Genesis 2:24: *"Therefore a man shall leave his father and his mother and hold fast to his wife, and they shall become one flesh."* This verse emphasizes the unity and permanence of the marital union, expressing God's intention for the bond between a husband and wife.

Traditional marriage vows that include the commitment 'till death do us part' reflect the understanding that marriage is a lifelong covenant, not to be broken except by the natural occurrence of death. They signify the depth of commitment, loyalty, and dedication that a couple promises to one another in the presence of God.

These vows are considered deeply meaningful and sacred, as they reflect the willingness to endure challenges, sacrifices, and growth as a couple. Keeping these vows requires effort, communication, forgiveness, and a commitment to working through difficulties.

It is important to note that while the concept of lifelong commitment is cherished by many, there are circumstances in which marriages may face irreconcilable issues or become harmful or abusive. In such cases, seeking professional help, counseling, or support is important for individuals facing difficult decisions regarding their marriages.

The significance of marriage vows and their endurance throughout history speaks to the value placed on the commitment and unity of a lifelong relationship.

This can include all aspects such as honoring marital commitments, promoting love and respect within the relationship, and prioritizing the well-being of the family unit. It is important to note, however, that different individuals and cultures may interpret divine order differently based on their specific religious beliefs and teachings. What constitutes divine order can vary even among different religious denominations or sects. Therefore, approach this concept with respect and recognize that diverse perspectives exist. When discussing marriage, it is valuable to engage in open dialogue, understanding, and empathy, acknowledging that people may have different interpretations of divine order.

"And the Lord God said, it is not good that the man should be alone; I will make him a help meet for him. (Wife)"

The quote above is provided from the Bible, specifically Genesis 2:18. In this passage, it is stated that God recognized that it was not good for Adam (the first man) to be alone and decided to create a suitable companion, referred to as a "help meet" or "helper" for him. This companion is traditionally understood to be a wife.

This passage from the Bible is often cited in discussions about the importance of companionship and the creation of marriage. It highlights the idea that marriage is a union where a husband and wife are intended to support and complement one another.

The vow 'until death do us part' emphasizes the significance of commitment, fidelity, and the intention to work through challenges and difficulties that may arise during a marriage. It reflects the belief that marriage is a lifelong commitment and that the couple is pledged to stay together until the end of their lives.

The biblical phrase, 'till death us do part' does not mean that any couple cannot separate if they choose to. The commitment and dedication required to make a marriage work to the best of one's ability. The emphasis here is the importance of trying to make it work. This implies that parting a marriage should only be for serious matters, not trivial ones.

Martial vows serve as a reminder of the gravity and seriousness of the commitment being made. We encourage couples to approach the challenges and difficulties that may arise in their marriage with a strong intention to work through them rather than giving up at the first sign of trouble. While dismissal and the possibility of separation or divorce in extreme circumstances, do encourage couples to view parting as a last resort and to prioritize their efforts to resolve conflicts and maintain a strong bond.

Each couple is encouraged to approach their marital commitment with a mindset of perseverance, growth, and shared responsibility. It is important to note that every marriage is unique, and there are situations where separation or divorce may be necessary for the well-being and safety of the individuals involved. In such cases, seeking professional advice is important.

While the phrase 'until death do us part' is often included in wedding vows, it is important for couples to understand that the commitment to their marriage goes beyond the words spoken during the ceremony. It extends to the daily choices, actions, and attitudes that couples adopt to honor and nurture their love for each other.

A strong and fulfilling marriage requires ongoing effort, communication, and mutual respect. It involves demonstrating love and commitment through actions, such as practicing kindness, forgiveness, and understanding toward one another.

Honoring the love between spouses involves prioritizing the relationship, investing time and energy into its growth, and supporting each other's personal and shared goals.

Couples should keep in mind that marriage is a dynamic journey that requires constant care and attention. It is important to cultivate a deep sense of mutual trust, open communication, and emotional connection.

Regularly expressing appreciation, showing affection, and actively listening to each other's needs and concerns are ways to honor the love shared between partners.

Moreover, honoring love also means weathering the storms and challenges that may arise in a marriage. It means being willing to work through conflicts, seek professional help when needed, and commit to the growth and transformation that can occur within the relationship.

The commitment to honor your love in a marriage is an ongoing process that requires dedication, effort, and continuous learning. By embracing this mindset and actively living out their commitment beyond the vows, couples can nurture and strengthen their love, fostering a lasting and fulfilling relationship.

'Until death do us part' is not limited to any specific religious context. Although it has biblical origins and is commonly associated with wedding vows in religious ceremonies, the underlying concept of committing to a lifelong relationship extends beyond any religious belief.

It represents a commitment to endure the nature of the marital bond, emphasizing the intention to stay together and support each other until death separates the couple. It reflects the idea of building a strong and lasting relationship based on love, trust, and mutual respect.

Regardless of religious affiliation, many couples embrace the concept of a lifelong commitment and strive to build stronger relationships based on shared values, effective communication, and dedication to one another. They recognize the importance of nurturing your relationship, working through challenges, and continuously investing in their connection.

The principle of 'until death do us part' serves as a foundation for building a stronger relationship by emphasizing the significance of commitment, loyalty, and perseverance. It encourages couples to prioritize their bond, prioritize the well-being and happiness of their spouse, and work together to overcome obstacles that may arise along the way.

While different couples may interpret and apply this principle in their unique ways, the fundamental idea of committing to a lifelong relationship and actively working towards a stronger relationship remains a common aspiration for many.

The concept of a soulmate is often associated with the belief that there is a special, destined person with whom one is meant to share a profound connection. It is believed by some that when two people are meant to be together as soulmates, their relationship is a destiny that will last.

In the context of a relationship that is ordained by God, it is believed by many religious individuals that when God brings two people together, their bond is strengthened and guided by a divine presence. This can provide a foundation of faith and spiritual connection that can help sustain and strengthen their relationship. It is important to note that the idea of soulmates and relationships ordained by God can be subjective interpretations.

Relationships, regardless of whether they are perceived as soulmate connections or believed to be divinely guided, still require effort, commitment, and continuous nurturing. Even in relationships that are believed to be deeply special or ordained, challenges can arise, and both partners need to actively work together to navigate and overcome them.

It is also important to acknowledge that not all relationships are meant to be lifelong, and sometimes individuals may experience multiple meaningful connections and relationships.

throughout their lives. The path and duration of a relationship can be influenced by various factors, including individual choices, personal growth, and external circumstances.

In conclusion, whether a relationship is believed to be a soulmate connection or guided by a divine presence, it is essential for both partners to invest in communication, understanding, and mutual respect in building a strong and lasting bond.

"TESTIMONIES"

I was married to my high school sweetheart; it was an ideal relationship. Well, as far as I was concerned. We were inseparable as a couple. Everyone that knew us expresses these sentiments exactly. By the way, my name is Victoria Williams, and my husband is Ron Williams. From our "union," we share four children. We have been happily married for over fifteen years. We shared everything. Including but not limited to vacationing with the family, working very well with each other in building up our home. We even took out time to care for our babies together. Nothing lacking, our attention concerning our family! We were in 'Love.'

One day we noticed our compassion beginning to diminish rapidly. What was once a perfect relationship turned into an uncomfortable odd lifestyle. Just to be a little candid: What happened? Why us? What did we miss? Why couldn't we see the issues that were destroying our marriage forthcoming? Maybe we were blinded by our overwhelming love for each other. Love can be blinding! After putting our efforts back into reconciling our marriage, we decided that we needed some professional 'Help.'

One of our associates suggested that we would speak with their Pastor, Dr. Brenda, and Bishop Andrew Harper. They expressed that they are some excellent counselors in "Marriage Counseling." We took their advice. Did I mention we were a year into our divorce? The "Authors" coached my husband and me back into the original spark of our marriage, and we renewed our "VOWS." I need to say, that they counseled us in such a loving way. We conceived our fourth child, a baby girl. We know this book, "God Ordains Marriages" will be a blessing to all couples. We suggest you apply the principles of this book!

The Williams Family…

Ms. V. Williams

GOD ORDAINS MARRIAGES

INDEX FOR FOUNDATIONS

CHAPTER 1

- Foundation of Jesus Christ
  - o This is always the foundational prayer for our family.
- A strong foundation of shared values and beliefs
  - o Rooted in faith in Christ
    - One of trust
    - Respect
    - Love
  - o Supportive relationship

CHAPTER 2

- Knowledge and understanding in a relationship
- Mutual respect
  - o Trust and commitment
  - o Self-evaluation
  - o Personal growth
- Strong and stable
  - o Open and honest communication
  - o Setting shared goals and values
  - o Resolving conflicts in a healthy way
  - o Spending quality time together

- o Supporting each other
- Universal principles
  - o Effective communication
  - o Mutual respect
  - o Trust
  - o Honesty
  - o Empathy
  - o Ability to compromise.
- "Strong and stable foundation"
  - o Time
  - o Effort
  - o Commitment
  - o Open communication
- Willingness to work through challenges and difficult times.
- Financial foundation
  - o Time and effort
  - o Panning
  - o Communication
  - o Willingness to work together

CHAPTER 3

Foundation of communication

CHAPTER 6

- Foundation for a thriving and fulfilling marriage
  - o Seeking unity
  - o Agreement
  - o Guarding against division

CHAPTER 7

- Financial foundation

- o Discussing the family budget
     Making joint decisions
- o Mindful of spending
- strong bond...Chapters 7, 9, and 10
  - o Sense of security
  - o Trust
  - o Emotional connection

CHAPTER 8

- Fulfillment and love
- Sacrifice and uncertainty
  - o Trust and faith
  - o Emotional investment
  - o Shared responsibility
  - o Growth and adaptation
       Commitment and perseverance
- Sacrifices and commitment
  - o Flexibility and adaptability
  - o Communication and collaboration
  - o Mutual support and understanding
  - o Shared responsibility
  - o Financial transparency and planning
  - o Mutual growth and fulfillment
- Maintaining unity (financial circumstances)
  - o Open communication
  - o Shared financial responsibility
  - o Budgeting and financial planning
  - o Support and understanding
  - o Adaptability and resourcefulness
  - o Focus on non-material aspects.
- Trust
  - o Open and honest communication
  - o Follow through on commitments

- o Support each other's goals.
- o Share responsibilities and make joint decisions.
- o Be reliable in small matters.
- o Be vulnerable and empathetic.
- o Patience and forgiveness
- Sacrifice
  - o Vulnerability and selflessness
  - o Reliability and consistency
  - o Mutual understanding of empathy
  - o Increased engagement
  - o Reciprocity and mutual support

"Establishing a solid foundation in various aspects of your lives can create a nurturing and fulfilling environment for both you and your future children."

CHAPTER 9

- Happiness and well-being
  - o Nurturing personal growth
    - Self-exploration
    - Pursuing passions
  - o Mental and emotional well-being
    - Self-care
    - Emotional resilience
  - o Establishing stronger relationships
    - Partner or spousal connection
    - Supportive network
  - o Financial stability
    - Achieving financial goals
- The foundation of marriage and family
  - o Love
  - o Support
  - o Shared experiences

- - Personal growth
  - Wellbeing
- Faith and Biblical principles
  - Guidance in navigating
    - Relationships
    - Family dynamics
  - Context
  - Lessons learned
  - Biblical foundation
    Respect individual differences
  - Encourage dialogue

CHAPTER 10

  - Biblical principles of family and marriage
    personal values
  - Faith
  - Marriage
  - Family
- Until death do us part
  - Emphasizing the significance of commitment
  - Loyalty
  - Perseverance
- Faith
- Spiritual connection (Chapters 7 and 10) for building a
  stronger relationship
  - Emphasizing the significance of commitment
  - Loyalty
  - Perseverance
- The foundation of faith and spiritual connection

ABOUT THE AUTHOR

 Apostle Dr. Brenda Harper is a motivational speaker and an influential teacher.

Dr. Harper along with her husband Chief Apostle Andrew Harper are the founders of AACTS International Ministries, Inc., where she serves as the Senior Pastor, under her husband the Overseer! In the beautiful City of Temecula, CA.

Her passion is to see great signs and wonders through the manifestation of the Holy Ghost, as she yields her vessel, unto the Lord. She desires to see souls restored unto the Lord, which has resulted in spiritual deliverance and miraculous healing.

Dr. Harper is the author of several books and holds serval degrees: Doctorate in Divinity & Theology, from Grace and Truth University. Doctorate in Psychology from Liberty University, and a Ph.D. in Philosophy, from Next Dimension University (NDU). She was the Dean of Five-Fold Ministry Theological University (FMTU), at San Diego State University. The first Satellite Director of The House of the Lord Theological Seminary (HOLT).

Mark 16:17-18